Welcome to New Orleans

French Quarter

Getting to New Orleans

BY PLANE

Louis Armstrong Airport (*900 Airline Dr., Kenner, LA; 001 504 464 0831; www.flymsy.com*) services the New Orleans Area. It's small and relatively easy to navigate. The city has began construction on a second terminal, with plans to open in 2019.

BY CAR

The 1-10 connects New Orleans to the surrounding region. From the east coast, take 1-10W toward Baton Rouge. From the west, Texas and Baton Rouge, take 1-10E towards New Orleans. Exit at 235A for the French Quarter.

BY BUS OR TRAIN

Both the Greyhound Bus Terminal and Union Train Station are located on Loyala Ave., just off of the Pontchartrain Expressway, in downtown New Orleans. Several train lines connect New Orleans to other major US cities.

New Orleans Union Passenger Terminal - *1001 Loyola Ave - 001 800 872 7245 - www.amtrak.com*

Greyhound - *1001 Loyola Ave - 001 504 524-7571 - www.greyhound.com*

Taxi Services - The airport is about 25 25 min from downtown New Orleans/ Canal St. Cabs charge a flat rate of $35. Rideshare services like Uber and Lyft charge comparable rates.

Streetcar, Bus and Public Transit - The E-2 bus line connects the airport with downtown New Orleans (every 30 min., $1.25). Once downtown, the bus line connects to several streetcar lines.

Jazzy Pass

1, 2, 3 or 5 -day passes (for streetcar and bus) may save you money on transport *p. 118.*

Crescent City Connection

Unmissable

Our picks for must-see sites:

French Market ★
Map F 5 - p. 20

City Park★★
Map CD 2 3 - p. 36

Jackson Square★★
p. 17

Audubon Park★★
Map AB 7 - p. 33

Magazine Street★★
Map DE 6 7 - p. 28

Royal Street★★
p. 20

National WWII Museum★★
Map E 6 - p. 26

Mardi Gras World★★★
Map F 6 - p. 32

Lafayette Cemetery★
Map D 7 - p. 30

Frenchmen Street★★
Map F 5 - p. 44

Our top picks

Immerse yourself in history in the nation's official World War II Museum. Afterwards, walk over to **Cochon** for a hearty dinner (or more casual lunch at **Cochon Butcher** next door). *See p.26.*

Ride the St. Charles streetcar from Canal St. to **Audubon Park**, and get a real sense for the city's crescent shape. From the trolley's windows, view 18C historic mansions and handsome hundreds-year-old live oak trees.

Get lost in the vast grounds of **City Park**, home to some of the oldest live oak trees in the city, the **Bestoff Sculpture Garden**, **Botanical Gardens**, and the **New Orleans Museum of Art (NoMA)**. Take a break on the veranda of **Morning Call** with a cafe au lait and plate of beignets.

Step back in time with a *Sazerac* or *Ramos Gin Fizz* at the **Sazerac Bar** inside the **Roosevelt Hotel**. The barroom has seen the likes of Louisiana Governor Huey P. Long, Frank Sinatra, Judy Garland and Marilyn Monroe.

Stroll **Magazine St.**, lined with the city's finest boutiques, antique stores, and galleries. End at an award-winning restaurant like Shaya or Le Petite Grocery.

Tour the ornate above-ground graves at cemeteries Louis #1 or Lafayette. Join a tour group to hear the full history of New Orleans' above-ground graves.

Explore the duality of the **French Quarter** with a walk both down the elegant **Royal St.**, of antique stores and galleries, and the neon lights and cheap thrills of **Bourbon St.**

Enjoy the sunset, a bottle of wine and live music in the backyard at Bacchanal in the Bywater.

Come nightfall, wander down **Frenchmen St.**, when it fills with music lovers and brass bands can be heard from the doorways of the jam-packed music clubs.

Take your place in the long line of locals waiting for po' boys at their favorite spots and, in spring and summer, for sno balls (sugary syrup-filled balls of shaved ice).

Live music at d.b.a., Frenchmen Street

Experience the best of New Orleans food, music, and revelry at **Mardi Gras**, **Jazz Fest**, or one of the city's many smaller, often free festivals throughout the year.

Look for more free, outdoor music on the corners of French Quarter streets, outside of the **French Market**, **Jackson Square**, and in the clubs of Frenchmen St..

In the spring, head to the nearest bar, seafood stand or neighborhood party for a sack of spicy boiled crawfish. *See New Orleans Cuisine p.43.*

Splurge on a decadent three-course lunch at the grand and historic Commander's Palace. Enter Lafayette Cemetery across the street for an after-lunch wander through the picturesque cemetery, inspiration for movies and Southern gothic novels.

Immerse yourself in the swamplands (and watch for alligators) at Fontainebleau State Park or Barrataria Preserve. *See p.95.*

New Orleans in 3 days

When heading out for a day of sightseeing, prepare for the Gulf South's often tempermental weather habits: carry water for heat, long sleeves for air-conditioned stores and museums, and an umbrella for the occasional downpour.

DAY 1

Morning

Begin your day with cafe au lait and beignets at the famous **Cafe Du Monde**, then walk alongside the food and knick-knack stands at the French Market. Spend the morning exploring one or two of the eclectic **museums** of the French Quarter: The Pharmacy Museum, Voodoo Museum, or Museum of Death.

Afternoon

For lunch, bite into a traditional muffaletta sandwich at **Central Grocery** before walking it off on Royal St., popping into art galleries.

Evening

Plan to spend an evening enjoying the music of the French Quarter. Wait in line at preservation hall, then walk along Bourbon St. as long as you can stand it, making your way to the musically-superior Frenchmen St. Depending on your taste, pop in for a set at The Spotted Cat, Cafe Negril or Snug Harbor.

DAY 2

Morning

Schedule a colorful ghost tour, architecture tour or cemetery tour of the French Quarter or Garden District.

Afternoon

Take the street car (Rampart St. line) or walk to the Faubourg Marigny/ Bywater neighborhood for lunch at one of its colorful cafes. Tour the socially-charged giant murals at StudioBe in the Bywater.

Late afternoon and evening

After a coffee and pastry break at **Bywater Bakery**, stroll through the colorful architecture and landscapes of the residential bywater neighborhood, ending along the Mississippi River at **Crescent City Park**.

After a glass of wine and dinner in the peaceful courtyards of Bacchanal or N7, choose from a variety of nightlife entertainment, like burlesque, karaoke and stand-up comedy, at the clubs and venues along St. Claude Avenue.

DAY 3

Morning

Begin with a central business district **museum** of choice: The World War II Museum, Ogden Museum of Southern Art or Confederate Museum Hall. Hop on the streetcar heading Uptown

Backyard, Bacchanal

toward the Garden District and take in views of the city's historic Antebellum mansions.
Exit the streetcar at Audubon Park for a romp through its picturesque grounds, ideal for bird watching. For lunch, bring a **picnic** to the Fly, a section of the park overlooking the river, where barges and cruise ships ply the water.

Afternoon and evening
From Audubon Park, make the short trip over to the **Carrolton Riverbend** of Uptown for two historic nightlife experiences: an indulgent creole dinner at **Jaques-Imo's** and a late night of the best local music at the **Maple Leaf Bar.**

If you have an extra day

From the end of Canal Street, take the ferry across the Mississippi River to explore historic Algier's Point, New Orleans' second oldest neighborhood, with charming architecture, cafes and great views of the French Quarter and downtown New Orleans across the river.
p.118.

NO
FIRE LANE

Discovering New Orleans

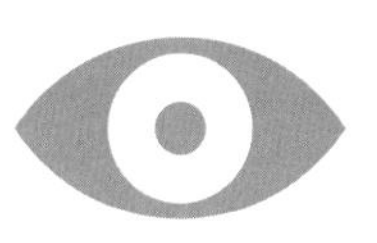

Royal Street, French Quarter

New Orleans today

In its topography, architecture, people and music, New Orleans resembles no other American city. Straddling the Mississippi River in southeastern Louisiana, the metropolis lies an average of 5ft below sea level. Its naturally swampy lands—laced with secondary tributaries called bayous—are made livable by an extensive system of levees, pumping stations and drainage canals. The city's long succession of inhabitants—encompassing the Native American indigenous population, French Creole and Spanish colonists, West Indian and African slaves, and settlers from Europe and the eastern US—has created a rich mix of peoples and cultures. The city's distinctive architecture is the result of European ideas adapted to the subtropical climate.

Visiting New Orleans

Its colorful cultural ambience, excellent restaurants and nowhere-else-but-here traditions make New Orleans one of the most popular tourist destinations in the US. Creativity, romance, drama and fun are always encouraged here. The American music form of jazz was born in Sunday-afternoon slave assemblages at Congo Square, then refined in the ballrooms, brothels and riverboats of the early 20C city; today the annual New Orleans Jazz & Heritage Festival (Jazzfest) attracts hundreds of thousands of music fans. Recovery continues from the effects of Hurricane Katrina, which struck the Gulf Coast in 2005 and caused the levee system around New Orleans to fail, inundating nearly 80 percent of the city and displacing tens of thousands of residents. Tourist attractions are fully restored to their pre-Katrina state, and most residential areas are on their way to full recovery. New Orleans received a huge boost when its beloved New Orleans Saints football team won the 2009 Super Bowl, and the annual Mardi Gras celebration in February remains a world-renowned event. The storied Superdome covered sports arena, less than 3mi west of downtown, has hosted half a dozen NFL championship Super Bowl football games. But, over a decade after Katrina, there are small reminders throughout the city of the devastation the storm left in its wake.

Celebrating 300 Years

2018 marks the city's tricentennial, 300 years since the 1718 founding of New Orleans. Aside from citywide restoration projects, events and celebrations throughout the city highlight different cultural aspects of its 300 years. View a calendar of events and project information on www.2018nola.com.

HERITAGESTAG

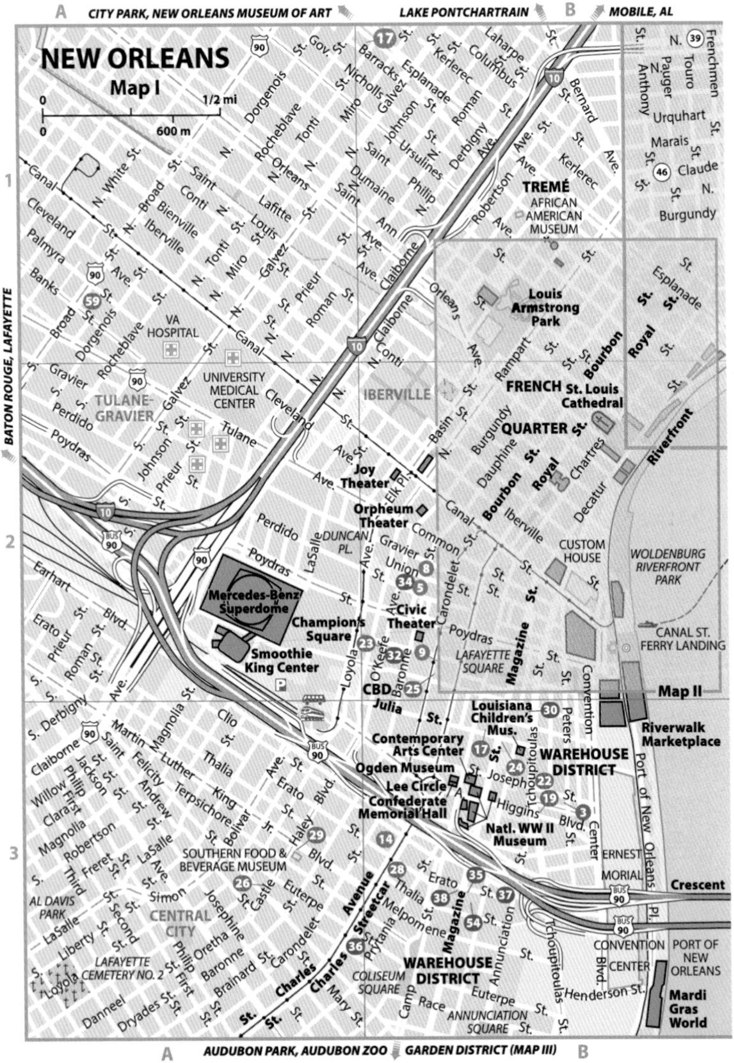
NEW ORLEANS
Map I
0
1/2 mi
0
600 m
A
B
1
2
3
CITY PARK, NEW ORLEANS MUSEUM OF ART
LAKE PONTCHARTRAIN
MOBILE, AL
BATON ROUGE, LAFAYETTE
AUDUBON PARK, AUDUBON ZOO
GARDEN DISTRICT (MAP III)
TREMÉ
AFRICAN AMERICAN MUSEUM
Louis Armstrong Park
FRENCH QUARTER
St. Louis Cathedral
Riverfront
IBERVILLE
TULANE-GRAVIER
VA HOSPITAL
UNIVERSITY MEDICAL CENTER
Joy Theater
Orpheum Theater
DUNCAN PL.
Mercedes-Benz Superdome
Champion's Square
Smoothie King Center
Civic Theater
LAFAYETTE SQUARE
CBD
CUSTOM HOUSE
WOLDENBURG RIVERFRONT PARK
CANAL ST. FERRY LANDING
Map II
Riverwalk Marketplace
Louisiana Children's Mus.
Contemporary Arts Center
Ogden Museum
Lee Circle
Confederate Memorial Hall
Natl. WW II Museum
WAREHOUSE DISTRICT
ERNEST MORIAL
Crescent
CONVENTION CENTER
PORT OF NEW ORLEANS
Mardi Gras World
SOUTHERN FOOD & BEVERAGE MUSEUM
AL DAVIS PARK
CENTRAL CITY
LAFAYETTE CEMETERY NO. 2
COLISEUM SQUARE
ANNUNCIATION SQUARE
St. Charles Avenue Streetcar
Canal St.
Claiborne Ave.
Esplanade Ave.
Rampart St.
Bourbon St.
Royal St.
Chartres St.
Decatur St.
Poydras St.
Magazine St.
Tchoupitoulas St.
Convention Center Blvd.
Julia St.
Carondelet St.
Loyola Ave.
Tulane Ave.
Earhart Blvd.
Martin Luther King Jr. Blvd.
Oretha Castle Haley Blvd.
Henderson St.
Port of New Orleans Pl.

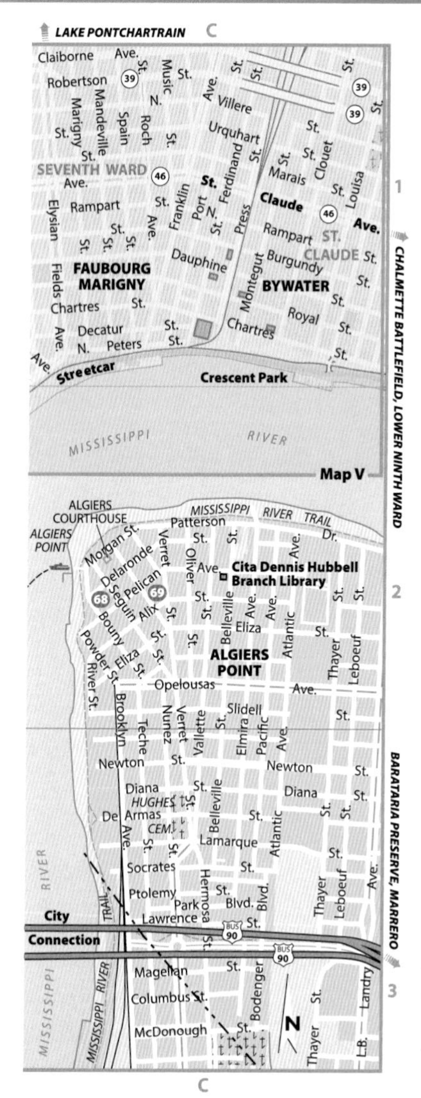

A Bit of History

New Orleans was founded in 1718 by French explorer Jean-Baptiste Le Moyne, sieur de Bienville, in an effort to solidify French claims in the New World. The site he chose, atop a naturally raised embankment along the Mississippi, was militarily and economically important as the gateway to the Louisiana Territory, but proved inauspicious for settlement. French engineers laid out a town plan in 1721, and early colonists (forerunners of the city's non-indigenous Creole population) battled hurricanes, floods and epidemics as they maintained the trappings of French society in the muddy outpost. In 1769 the city came under Spanish rule, but was returned to France in 1803. A month later Napoleon sold the entire Louisiana Territory including New Orleans to the US for approximately $15 million.

The decades following the Louisiana Purchase saw an explosion in the city's population as settlers flooded west to occupy the new American territory. New Orleans grew to be the fourth-largest city in the US by 1840, its prosperity buoyed by the river trade. Shunned by the Creoles, Anglo-American newcomers settled in suburbs upriver from the French Quarter. Staunchly Confederate on the eve of the Civil War, New Orleans capitulated to a Union takeover in 1862 and was spared destruction.

The 20C saw numerous improvements to public-works systems, most importantly the development of flood-control measures that

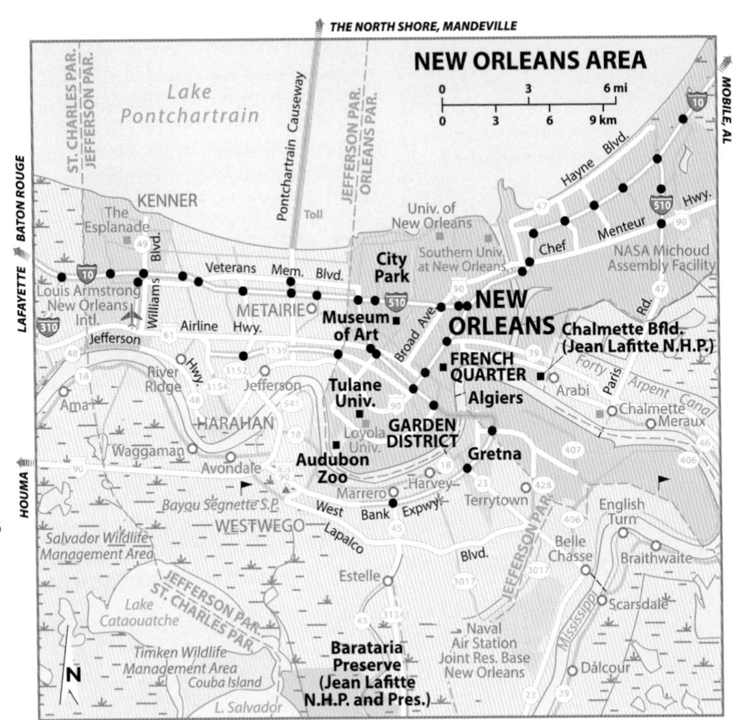

diverted river swells into shallow Lake Pontchartrain north of the city. The discovery of oil beneath the waters of the Gulf of Mexico brought new economic prosperity, along with continued port activities and increasingly, tourism.

Katrina and Recovery

At the end of August 2005, vast areas of New Orleans were flooded due to catastrophic levee breaches after Hurricane Katrina, bringing devastation to many of the city's poorer neighborhoods. Like most parts of town developed before the late 19C, the historic French Quarter escaped relatively unscathed, with most businesses able to reopen within two months. Other residential areas of the city, particularly New Orleans East, the Lower Ninth Ward, and St. Bernard Parish continue to recover, with rebuilding programs ongoing.

The French Quarter★★★

Historically known as the Vieux Carré, the fabled rectangle that for many embodies the essence of New Orleans, the French Quarter occupies roughly 100 blocks bounded by Canal Street, Rampart Street, Esplanade Avenue, and the great curve of the Mississippi River. The grid pattern laid out in 1721 survives today, but devastating fires in 1788 and 1794 wiped out most early French colonial constructions. The distinctive architectural flavor of the French Quarter—with its stucco surfaces in bright pastel tints, intricately patterned cast-iron galleries and secluded interior courtyards—developed during the city's Spanish and early American periods. New Orleans' French Creole population remained firmly entrenched here from the city's earliest days through the Civil War and Reconstruction, but by the late 19C an influx of immigrants had moved in and the genteel quarter became a rowdy commercial and nightlife district. Today most Quarter residents live quietly behind the closed shutters of Creole cottages and town houses lining the streets on the lake side of Bourbon Street and downriver of Dumaine. But on Bourbon, Royal and Decatur Streets, on the broad pedestrian malls surrounding Jackson Square, and on the plazas near the French Market, the vibrant public life of the Quarter plays out daily like an urban musical comedy.

▶**Access:** #47 and #48-Canal Streetcar, #49-Rampart Streetcar lines-#5, #55 Buses at St. Peter-Mississippi River Ferry at Canal Street.

Area map p. 16-17. Detachable map EF5-6.

▶**Tips:** Opt for the areas around Chartres Street and Royal Street instead of the busier, tourist-trap areas of Canal and Bourbon Streets.

JACKSON SQUARE★★

F6 *Bounded by Chartres, St. Philip, Decatur & St. Ann Sts.*

Laid out as a military parade ground known as Place d'Armes, the fenced and landscaped square at the foot of Orleans Street was renamed in 1851 to honor Andrew Jackson (1767-1845), hero of the Battle of New Orleans and seventh US president. The monumental statue of Jackson astride a rearing horse was dedicated in 1856. Surrounded by elegant **St. Louis Cathedral★** (1794), government buildings and the 1840s **Pontalba Buildings★**, the square served as the focal point of the old city; today street performers, artists and vendors set up shop on the square's flagstone perimeter. Across Decatur Street downriver from the square, Café du Monde serves up café au lait and beignets (square donuts dredged in powdered sugar). Opposite looms handsome

LOUISIANA STATE MUSEUM CABILDO

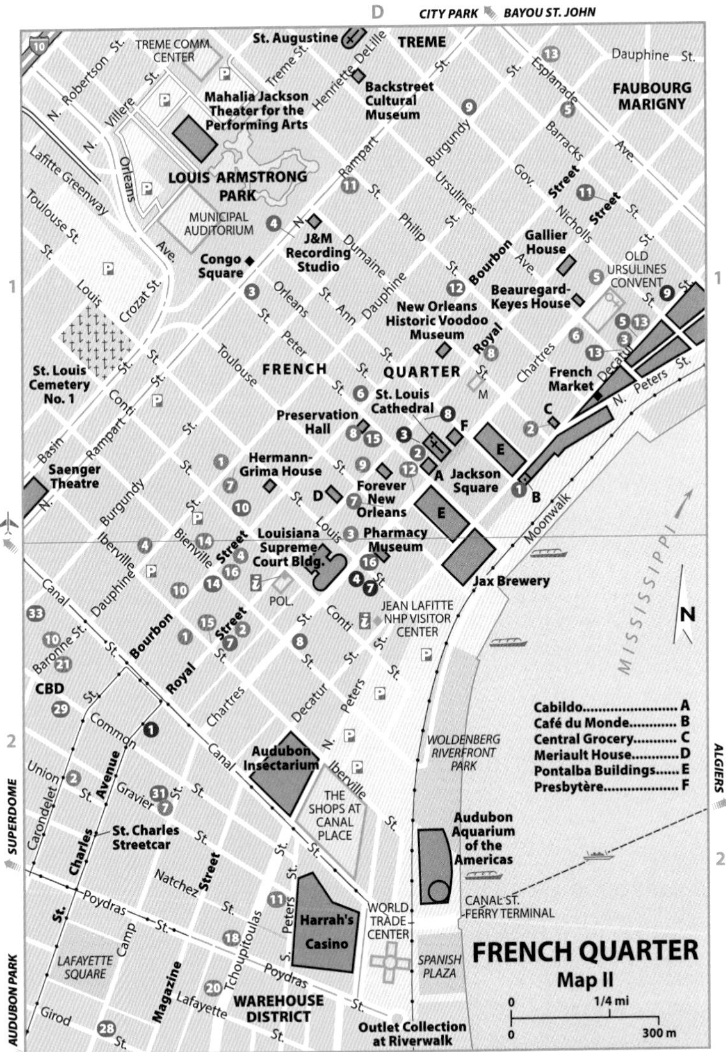
FRENCH QUARTER
Map II
Cabildo........................ A
Café du Monde............ B
Central Grocery........... C
Meriault House............ D
Pontalba Buildings...... E
Presbytère................... F
CITY PARK
BAYOU ST. JOHN
TREME
FAUBOURG MARIGNY
LOUIS ARMSTRONG PARK
FRENCH QUARTER
St. Augustine
Backstreet Cultural Museum
Mahalia Jackson Theater for the Performing Arts
TREME COMM. CENTER
MUNICIPAL AUDITORIUM
J&M Recording Studio
Congo Square
St. Louis Cemetery No. 1
Saenger Theatre
Gallier House
OLD URSULINES CONVENT
Beauregard-Keyes House
New Orleans Historic Voodoo Museum
French Market
St. Louis Cathedral
Preservation Hall
Hermann-Grima House
Forever New Orleans
Jackson Square
Louisiana Supreme Court Bldg.
Pharmacy Museum
Jax Brewery
JEAN LAFITTE NHP VISITOR CENTER
Moonwalk
MISSISSIPPI
WOLDENBERG RIVERFRONT PARK
Audubon Insectarium
THE SHOPS AT CANAL PLACE
Audubon Aquarium of the Americas
CANAL ST. FERRY TERMINAL
St. Charles Streetcar
Harrah's Casino
WORLD TRADE CENTER
SPANISH PLAZA
LAFAYETTE SQUARE
WAREHOUSE DISTRICT
CBD
Outlet Collection at Riverwalk
SUPERDOME
AUDUBON PARK
ALGIERS
NATIONAL WWII MUSEUM, GARDEN DISTRICT, OGDEN MUSEUM OF SOUTHERN ART, AUDUBON ZOO
1/4 mi
300 m

Jax Brewery, erected in 1891 and now renovated as a mall. A stairway between the two leads to the Moonwalk, a boarded promenade where visitors can watch ships navigating the bend in the Mississippi that gave rise to New Orleans' nickname "the Crescent City."
For a view of the city from the Mississippi River, take one of the paddlewheeler cruises that depart from the waterfront upriver from Jackson Square.

CABILDO★★

***E5** 701 Chartres St. - ✆ 504 568 6968- www.louisianastatemuseum.org - 10am-4:30pm - Closed Mondays - $6.*
To the left of the cathedral stands the Cabildo, erected by the Spanish government in 1799; the papers completing the territory transfers of the Louisiana Purchase were signed here in 1803. Today the handsome building and the adjacent Arsenal contain excellent displays of Louisiana history; on view here is one of the four original bronze death masks made of Napoleon in 1821.
Complementing the Cabildo to the right of the cathedral, the 1813 **Presbytère**★★ was built to house the bishops of Louisiana; today it showcases Katrina & Beyond, a sobering exhibit leading visitors through New Orleans residents' experience of the natural disaster that will forever mark the city. The upper level houses an exhibition about the colorful history of Mardi Gras in New Orleans.

FRENCH MARKET★

***E5** 1008 N. Peters St.- ✆504 522 2621 - www.frenchmarket.org - daily 7am-7pm.*
Extending downriver from Jackson Square, this bustling marketplace (1813) served the daily needs of New Orleans' Creole population. Stores (mostly gift shops) and restaurants occupy the structures today; the building remains open to the air, as it was in the 19C, and populated by vendors selling tables of crafts and flea-market wares.
Step across Decatur Street to the old **Central Grocery** (*923 Decatur St.*) and pick up a muffuletta, the pungent New Orleans sandwich made of Italian deli meats and cheeses layered on round bread and spiked with chopped-olive salad. But be sure to have plenty of napkins on hand.

ROYAL STREET★★

***E5** 100-1300 Royal St. - Between Canal St. and Esplanade Ave. - A block south of Bourbon St.*
Elegant Royal Street is best-known for the many shops and galleries occupying the street-level façades of its early-19C town houses. It is a street for meandering, with pauses to poke through galleries and to gaze upward at intricately whorled galleries of wrought and cast iron.
The massive white marble and granite **Louisiana Supreme Court Building (no. 400)**, was completed in 1910.
Selections from the holdings at the **Historic New Orleans Collection**★ (*✆504 523 4662; www.hnoc.org*)

© Zack Smith Photography/New Orleans Convention and Visitors Bureau

Royal Street

furnish changing exhibits presented in the ground-floor gallery of the **1792 Merieult House** at no. 533. Departing from the **Forever New Orleans shop** (*no. 624; ℘504 568 1801; www.mondecreole.com*), **Le Monde Creole** conducts excellent guided walking toursa that access several romantic interior courtyards while illustrating the intricacies of the city's French and West African Creole society.

You can tour the **Gallier House★** (*nos. 1118-1132; ℘504 274 0748; www.hgghh.org*), a fine example of Creole and American style elements; the same organization offers tours of the beautifully restored Federal-style **Hermann-Grima House** (*820 St. Louis St.; ℘504 274 0750*).

BOURBON STREET★

Year-round, but especially during Mardi Gras, Bourbon Street teems with cocktail-toting revelers who come to celebrate, drown their sorrows or simply indulge in the pleasures of this unabashedly hedonistic city. Lights flash, music booms and hawkers stand in doorways touting the dubious wanton pleasures within.

Some of the finest traditional jazz is performed nightly at 8pm, 9pm and 10pm just off Bourbon at **Preservation Hall★★** (*726 St. Peter St.; ℘504 522 2841; www.preservationhall.com*), one of the city's best-known and historic jazz venues.

Walking Tours of the French Quarter

Walking Tour: *(504 503 0199 - www.neworleanslegendarywalkingtours.com)*
Choose from a French Quarter and cemetery tour, a Garden District mansions tour, or ghost tour--or make time for them all. All walking tours come with guides knowledgeable on New Orleans history, architecture, and legends.
Ghost Tour: *(504 861 2727 - www.hauntedhistorytours.com)*
Enthusiast tour guides, serious about all things haunted and experts on the spookiest legends around town, guide you through a dramatic tour of the French Quarter's most haunted quarters, with stories peppering the walk. The standard tour is $25.
Cocktail Tour: *(www.graylineneworleans.com/all/tours/cocktail-tour) $31 per person (tour comes with one free cocktail); must be 21 years old.- this festive tour gives an introduction to the most famous classic new orleans cocktails, and where to drink them.*
Music Tour: *(www.acloserwalknola.com). Local radio station, WWOZ, maps out different (self-guided) tours, providing guided information of musical landmarks throughout town.*

BEAUREGARD KEYES HOUSE

1113 Chartres St. - ✆504 523 7257 - www.bkhouse.org.
During the late 1940s, beloved American author Frances Parkinson Keyes (1885-1970) restored her gracious home, Beauregard-Keyes House, where she lived until the 1970s. The house had been the residence of Con-federate general P.G.T. Beauregard for 18 months following the Civil War. It now contains a collection of fans, folk costumes and more than 200 antique dolls.

NEW ORLEANS HISTORIC VOODOO MUSEUM

724 Dumaine St - ✆504-680-0128 - voodoomuseum.com - 10am-6pm.
Through mysterious artifacts and artwork, the New Orleans Historic Voodoo Museum provides glimpses into the world of voodoo, the occult religion that arrived in New Orleans with the slave trade, and continues to flourish today.

PHARMACY MUSEUM

514 Chartres St - ✆504 565-8027 - www.pharmacymuseum.org - 10am-4pm - Closed Sun and Mon - $5.
The French Quarter is famous for zany small museums, and this 1820s apothecary is among the most fun to explore. This is the former shop of the first licensed pharmacist in America. The walls are lined with glass bottles of potions, strange medicines and herbs; glass cabinets showcase bizarre medical tools used for somewhat unbelievable, improvised practices of the times, like blood-letting opium and voodoo potions. All is a reminder of a time when modern medicine was just beginning.

AUDUBON INSECTARIUM

423 Canal St. - ☏504 581 4629 - www.audubon institute.org - daily 10am-5pm - $22.95, children $17.95 (combo ticket to Zoo, Aquarium, Insectarium and Butterfly Garden $44.95, $34.95).

Like its sister Audubon institutions (the Aquarium and the Zoo), the Insectarium, which occupies the lower floor of the historic US Custom House, makes learning about the natural world fun. Bugs—their habits, their biology, and (in some cases) their flavor—are the focus of kid-oriented exhibits. Enticing interactive displays and lots of live specimens highlight the adaptability of nature's supreme survivors. Exhibit areas include the Louisiana Swamp, the Metamorphoses Gallery (where butterflies emerge regularly from racks of chrysalises) and the Termite Gallery. Stop in at the Bug Appetit cafe to sample snacks made of edible insects. The visit ends with a walk through the Butterflies in Flight Gallery, where 400 of the beautiful creatures flit, flutter and perch (sometimes on visitors!).

Audubon Aquarium of the Americas

AUDUBON AQUARIUM OF THE AMERICAS

1 Canal St. - ☏504-861-2537 - www.auduboninstitute.org - daily 10am-5pm - $29.95, children $21.95.

Innovative exhibits highlighting marine specimens from North, Central and South America delight visitors to the Aquarium of the Americas. This fine aquarium is distinguished by its slanted blue-green cylinder rising at the foot of Canal Street. Moray eels, silvery tarpon and other colorful creatures glide overhead as visitors navigate the walk-through tunnel of the Maya Reef. The aquarium's playful sea otters cavort in their see-through tank, while fearsome piranhas glide in the Amazon Rain Forest. The Mississippi River exhibit reveals a wealth of catfish, bass, crappies and a rare white alligator. Other features include Adventure Island, an interactive play zone for kids with a touch pool filled with bullnose and cownose rays; a colony of playful penguins; Parakeet Pointe, home to hundreds of colorful parakeets flitting in their free-flight exhibit; and an IMAX theater.

CBD and Warehouse District ★★★

The Central Business District, known informally as the CBD, meets the French Quarter at Canal Street and runs from the 1-10 underpass to the Mississippi River. While it is home to government buildings, large businesses and big box hotels, you'll find some of the finest dining in the city here, as well as museums and shops. The Warehouse district, the once-bland industrial sector extending upriver from Poydras Street, thrives as the center of visual arts in New Orleans. Warehouses that sprang up behind riverfront docks in the early 19C have been reborn as studios and museums while street-level storefronts along Julia Street house a variety of contemporary art galleries.

▶**Access: Streetcar lines** #47 and #48-Canal St., #49- Rampart St., #12-St. Charles Ave. Bus lines #11 (Camp St.) and #10, #11, #100 (Magazine St.).

Detachable map DE4-5.

▶**Tips:** The CBD caters to a working crowd: aside from hotels and a few fine dining restaurants. Businesses in the CBD close early, around 6pm, and are often closed or have shorter hours on weekends.

CONTEMPORARY ARTS CENTER

G5-6 *900 Camp St. - ✆504-528-3800 - www.cacno.org - daily 11am-5pm - closed Tues.*

Occupying a handsome former factory and warehouse, the CAC mounts live performances and edgy temporary exhibits of modern visual art in its sleekly renovated gallery spaces.

OUTLET COLLECTION AT RIVERWALK

G5-6 *500 Port of New Orleans - ✆504 522 1555 - www.riverwalkneworleans.com - daily 10am-9pm.*

A festive mall of discount chains and local specialty stores, shops here stretch along the area where riverfront loading docks once fringed the Mississippi (Poydras, Canal and Julia Sts.).

LOUISIANA CHILDREN'S MUSEUM

G5-6 *420 Julia St. - ✆504 523 1357 - www.lcm.org - 9am-4:30pm; Sundays 12pm-4:30pm; closed Mondays.*

This fine museum wows creative kids with its fun activities and displays like a pint-sized grocery store, a miniature art studio, a playground of simple machines and a giant bubble play area.

CONFEDERATE MEMORIAL HALL

G5-6 *929 Camp St. - ✆504 523 4522 - www.confederatemuseum.com - daily 10am-4pm - closed Sun. and Mon.* Within this Romanesque-style building (1891) is a nice collection of paintings, photographs, uniforms, battle memorabilia and other artifacts of the Civil War, including personal belongings of Robert E. Lee, Stonewall Jackson and Jefferson Davis.

OGDEN MUSEUM OF SOUTHERN ART

G5-6 *925 Camp St. - ✆504 539 9650 - www.ogdenmuseum.org - daily 10am-5pm.* The permanent collection at this museum is a mix of paintings,

© Paul Broussard/New Orleans Convention and Visitors Bureau

National WWII Museum

crafts and works in mixed-media. Watercolorist Walter Inglis Anderson, visionary artist Howard Finster and sculptor Ida Kohlmeyer are represented here along with studio glass from the Penland School.

NATIONAL WWII MUSEUM ★★

945 Magazine St. (entrance on Andrew Higgins Dr.) - ✆504 528 1944 - www.nationalww2museum.org
A sobering but ultimately inspirational experience, this museum occupies a complex of state-of-the-art facilities in the Warehouse District. Its exhibits presents the American experience of the most wide-ranging and transformative armed conflict in modern history. Displays about the enormously complicated amphibious landing operations that turned the tide of the war are the focus of the museum's earliest section. Expansions in recent years employ artifacts, fiber-optic maps, letters, personal articles, uniforms, and in particular photographs and videos, to detail the entire scope of the conflict from the expansionist policies of Germany, Italy and Japan in the 1930s through the US entry into the war in 1941 to the August 1945 dropping of the atomic bomb on Hiroshima.

Enter the grand Louisiana Memorial Pavilion where you'll see large artifacts, including a restored C-47 troop carrier aircraft and a Higgins boat, one of the shallow-draft 36-passenger transports—designed and built in New Orleans—credited by General Dwight D. Eisenhower with winning the war by enabling amphibious landings.

Throughout the main building, video stations continuously screen short films highlighting personal histories and major conflicts such as the battles of Midway, the Philippines and the Leyte Gulf.

Across the street, the museum's theater screens emotional 4-D presentation **Beyond all Boundaries**, featuring immersive special effects that plunge the viewer into the story of this war. In the Restoration Pavilion, visitors can see pieces from the museum's ever-expanding collection of large artifacts (boats, vehicles, weapons) undergoing restoration.

Exhibits in the Freedom Pavilion detail soldiers' lives as well as life on the homefront.

GALLERIES OF JULIA STREET

G5-6 *Julia Street, between Commerce St. and St. Charles Ave., in the Warehouse District - www.artsdistrictneworleans.com.*
Stroll these several blocks of Julia Street to find galleries showcasing the finest in contemporary New Orleans and Southern art.

MERCEDES BENZ SUPERDOME

G5-6 *1500 Sugarbowl Dr. - ✆504 587 3822 - www.mbsuperdome.com.*
New Orleanians and ardent Saints' fans will refer to a visit to the dome for a Sunday game as "going to church". The massive, steel-framed sports arena is completely covered, 13-acres wide, and seats over 70,000 people.

Saints tickets are typically sold by the season, but several resale sights will sell individual tickets at a slightly elevated price. Check the NFL Ticket Exchange at **www.ticketexchangebyticketmaster.com**. if you can't get a ticket, the area around the dome, with sports bars and large parties in parking lots and under the overpass, is a fun place to celebrate the local, beloved (though not always winning) team.

In front of the dome, **Champions Square** *(www.champions-square.com)* is home to game day pre-game celebrations and many festivals and outdoor concerts.

Next door, the **Smoothie King Center** *(www.smoothiekingcenter.com)* hosts large scale concerts.

HARRAH'S CASINO

G5-6 *8 Canal St. - ✆504 533 6000 - www.caesars.com/harrahs-new-orleans - Open 24/7.*
Many a winner (and loser) enter Harrah's at least once during a weekend to New Orleans. The massive casino provides a mecca of entertainment: smoke-free since 2015 (but with a smoking porch, complete with gaming options), the casino has over 1500 slots and 130 table games, several dining options, a cocktail lounge, and a nightclub.

The Garden District★

A rectangle formed by St. Charles Avenue, Jackson Avenue, Magazine Street and Louisiana Avenue, this verdant neighborhood includes an unmatched assortment of antebellum mansions (Greek Revival and Italianate styles predominate) erected mostly for Anglo-Saxon newcomers to New Orleans in the mid-19C. Built in the center of large plots of land, the houses allow space for front "gardens" where exotics such as banana, bougainvillea, magnolia, crape myrtle and oleander still flourish.

Access: The #12 streetcar line runs along St. Charles Ave. in both directions, from the CBD to Uptown/Audubon Park. On Magazine St., the neighborhood's other main thoroughfare, the #11 bus runs the length of the street in both directions.
Detachable map. 28-29. EG4-6.
Tips: Combine a walking tour of Garden District mansions and Lafayette Cemetery with a traditional Southern lunch at Commander's Palace or with dinner at one of the award-winning restuarants on Magazine St.

MAGAZINE STREET★★

G5-6
Five blocks toward the river from St. Charles Ave.- stretches from the CBD to Audubon Park.
This colorful commercial and residential thoroughfare winds its way from the Warehouse District to Audubon Park. The blocks are jammed with restaurants and coffeehouses, designer boutiques and second-hand stores, upscale furniture and import showrooms and gift shops of every stripe.

ST CHARLES AVENUE

G6
The historic streetcar on St. Charles Avenue has been running since 1835, when it was built in conjunction with the New Orleans and Carrollton Railroad. To visitors' delight, it still maintains much of its historic charm, and taking a seat on one of its wooden benches, while watching the scenery slowly pass by, is a delightful way to experience the neighborhood. Shops, cafés and restaurants, as well as some of the most gorgeous mansions and old buildings of the neighborhood, are all along this wide avenue. The streetcar runs on slightly elevated land in the middle of the avenue, the sight of one of the city's natural levees.

Starting from the CBD and heading toward the Lower Garden District, the mostly quiet avenue is littered with hotels, museums, restaurants and coffee shops. During Mardi Gras parades, families gather in this

2032
APPARTIQUE
APPAREL · ART · ANTIQUES
Bella Umbrella
MIETTE

Houses of the Garden District

neighborhood and around the former **Lee Circle** to watch parades and enjoy the revelry (Civil War General Robert E. Lee's statue stood at this traffic circle until 2017, when it was removed as part of an effort to rid the city of its Confederate monuments. The city is at work on a replacement monument). Under the 1-10 overpass at St. Charles Ave., marching bands stop during parades for extended musical performances.

The avenue continues through the Garden District, in the shade of gorgeous live oak trees, planted in the early 20th Century in conjunction with the avenue's grand mansions. Uptown, St. Charles passes Loyola and Tulane Universities (nos. 6363 and 6823) on the "upriver" side, and the entrance to Audubon Park. The avenue ends near Carrollton Avenue, at the Uptown bend of the Mississippi River.

LAFAYETTE CEMETERY★

F5 *- 1416-1498 Washington Ave. - ✆ 01 44 78 75 00 - www.saveourcemeteries.org - ♿ - daily 7am–3pm - Tours $15.*

Across the street from the colorful striped awnings of Commander's Palace restaurant, this 19C cemetery houses the above-ground graves and ornate stone statues characteristic of New Orleans.

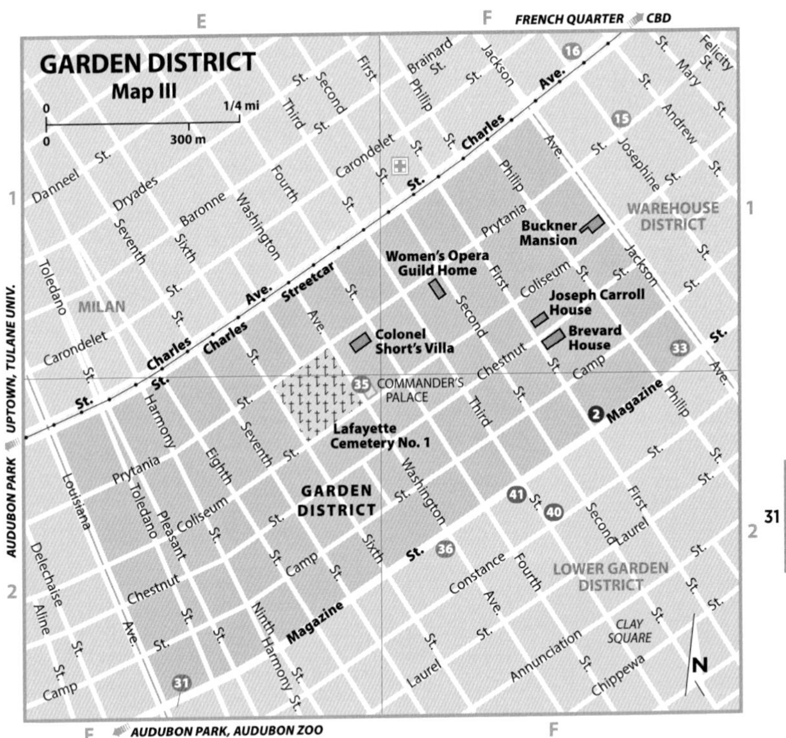

Established in 1833 during the planning for Lafayette City (now known as the Garden District), the still-active cemetery holds over 1,000 tombs and is the size of the city block. Anne Rice's Interview with a Vampire stole inspiration from graves here, and scenes from the movie Double Jeopardy and NCIS: New Orleans were filmed inside. The Save Our Cemeteries organization offers daily walking tours at 10:30am and 1:00pm.

MANSIONS OF THE GARDEN DISTRICT ★★

G6

Starting along **St. Charles Avenue** in the Garden District, and wandering among its early numbered streets and the residential Prytania Street one block downriver from St. Charles, will take you by some of the beautiful, historic mansions of the area.

Begin on First Street at the **Joseph Carroll House** (1315 First St.), an Italianite-style mansion built in 1869 for a Virginia cotton merchant, and notable for its octagonal wings. On the next block, you'll pass the Greek Revival-style **Brevard House** (*1239 First St.*). Shrouded in live oak trees, the double-galleried house was built in 1857 for a New Orleans Merchant. It's best known as the former house of novelist Anne Rice and is featured much in her haunting work.

Turning onto Prytania Street, make time to tour the **Women's Opera Guild Home** (*2504 Prytania St.; ℘504 267 9539; www.operaguildhome.org - open daily but tours Mon. 10am-4pm - $15*), a Greek Revival mansion donated to the Opera Guild in the 1960s .

© Gourmet Reise/New Orleans Convention and Visitors Bureau

Mardi Gras World

Explore the rest of the neighborhood and find for a glimpse at **Colonel Short's Villa** (*1448 Fourth St.*) an architectural wonder most famous for its cornstalk-shaped cast-iron fence.

Ghost lovers must make a stop at **Buckner Mansion** (*1410 Jackson Ave.*), especially at night. This Corinthian-columned behemoth of a mansion is the home of many rumored ghost stories. The 20,000 square-foot house, with three ballrooms, was constructed for the prideful Henry S. Buckner, a 19C cotton king. Now a rental house (for those with very large budgets!) the house was a recent setting for the television show **American Horror Story**.

MARDI GRAS WORLD★★★

G5 *1380 Port of New Orleans Pl. - ℘504 361 7821 - www.mardigrasworld.com - 9:30am-4:30pm - $22.* This massive warehouse-of-a museum takes you through the world of all things Mardi Gras, from traditions like king cake and beads, to how the floats are made and parades assembled. Touring the working warehouse, where you can see how and where most of the giant parade floats used during Mardi Gras are made, is a favorite kid-friendly attraction.

Uptown

Cradling a large western bend of Mississippi River, between Napoleon and Monticello Avenues, the name "Uptown" refers less to a neighborhood and more to the direction of the river's flow as you move away from downtown and the French Quarter. The area was home to many 19th Century (primarily Anglophone) settlers after the Louisiana Purchase, still evident by the many historic 19th Century mansions throughout the neighborhood. Today, sections of uptown (around Audubon Park) are home to some of the finest houses in New Orleans. On Magazine Street and other main thoroughfares you'll find restuarants and small businesses. Around Tulane and Loyola Universities, and the Carrolton Avenue-River Bend, the neighborhood turns into a college town, with burger joints, coffee shops and vintage stores catering to a young crowd.

▶**Access: Streetcar line:** #12-St. Charles Ave. (continues up Carrolton Avenue); Bus lines: #11 (Magazine St.) and #28 (Napoleon Ave.)

Area map p. 40-41. Detachable map EG6-8.

▶**Tip:** The neighborhood is too large to explore by foot. Plan to take a car or public transportation, or choose one day to explore Audubon Park and another for the Carrolton-Riverbend area.

AUDUBON ZOO

E6 *6500 Magazine St. - ✆504 861 2537 www.audubonnatureinstitute.org/zoo - daily 10am-4pm (5pm Sat. and Sun) - $22.95, children $17.95 - (combo ticket to Zoo, Aquarium, Insectarium and Butterfly Garden $44.95, $34.95).*

With its lush landscaping and exhibits featuring exotic animals from around the globe, this well-designed zoo is a treat. The Louisiana Swamp exhibit mimics life on the bayou and features fish, nutria, and a large group of alligators (including a rare white alligator). The Reptile House boasts a rare Komodo dragon, and Monkey Hill offers kids the chance to run and climb. Don't miss the daily giraffe and elephant feedings. On sweltering days, the Cool Zoo splash park offers welcome relief.

AUDUBON PARK★★

Bounded by St. Charles, Walnut & Calhoun Sts. - www.audubonnatureinstitute.org/audubon-park.

Across Magazine Street from the zoo lies **Audubon Park**. Formerly the site of a 400-acre sugar plantation, this space served as a Union encampment during the Civil War and as the site of the 1884 World's Cotton Centennial, which sparked residential development of uptown New Orleans. An oak-lined path curves along the

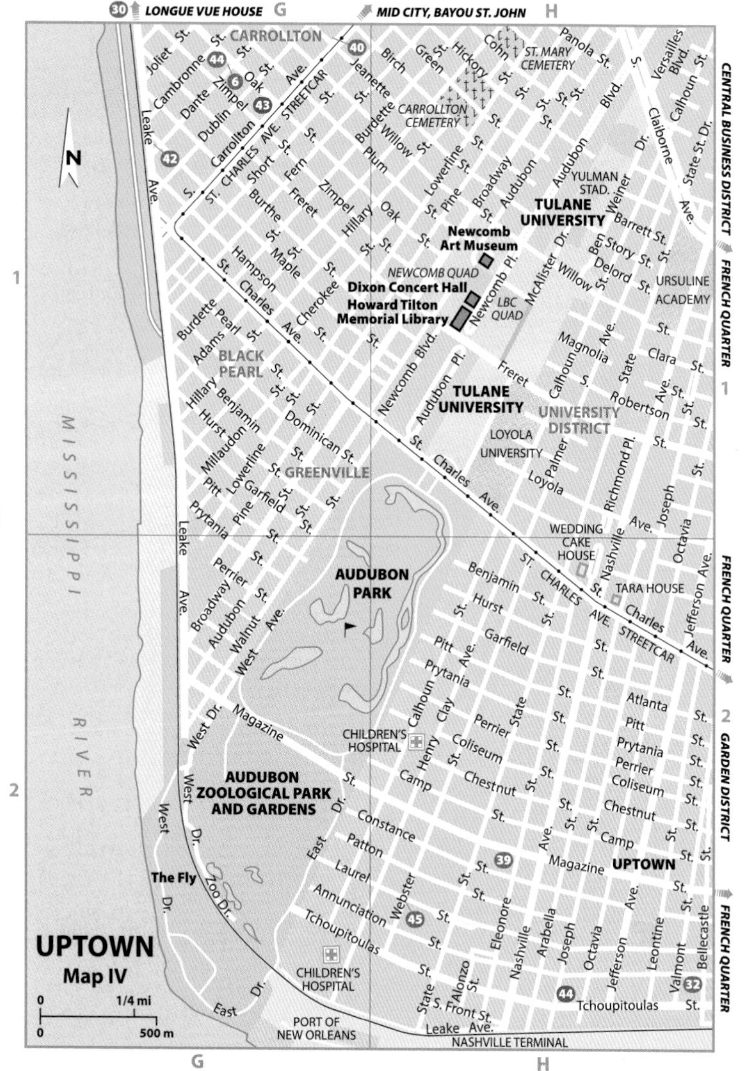
UPTOWN
Map IV
LONGUE VUE HOUSE
MID CITY, BAYOU ST. JOHN
CENTRAL BUSINESS DISTRICT
FRENCH QUARTER
GARDEN DISTRICT
MISSISSIPPI RIVER
CARROLLTON
ST. MARY CEMETERY
CARROLLTON CEMETERY
TULANE UNIVERSITY
YULMAN STAD.
Newcomb Art Museum
NEWCOMB QUAD
Dixon Concert Hall
Howard Tilton Memorial Library
LBC QUAD
URSULINE ACADEMY
BLACK PEARL
UNIVERSITY DISTRICT
LOYOLA UNIVERSITY
GREENVILLE
WEDDING CAKE HOUSE
TARA HOUSE
AUDUBON PARK
CHILDREN'S HOSPITAL
AUDUBON ZOOLOGICAL PARK AND GARDENS
The Fly
UPTOWN
PORT OF NEW ORLEANS
NASHVILLE TERMINAL
ST. CHARLES AVE. STREETCAR
0 1/4 mi
0 500 m

© Rauluminate/iStockphoto.com

Audubon Park

park perimeter around a golf course. Walk through the park and along the river until you reach **The Fly**, a popular spot for Tulane University students to play softball, volleyball and hang out in the grass along the river. This area of the park showcases a busy bend in the Mississippi, and is a great place to picnic while watching barges and cargo ships float by.

TULANE UNIVERSITY

***E6** 6823 St Charles Ave - www.tulane.edu.* This private school was founded in 1834 as a medical college and today is considered Louisiana's top university.

Special collections at the recently renovated **Howard Tilton Memorial Library** (*7001 Freret St. - ℘504 865 5605 - www.library.tulane.edu)* include archives and rare books on early American history, jazz, and Louisiana architecture.

The Tulane Performing Arts department hosts jazz and classical concerts, plays and an annual Shakespeare festival at **Dixon Concert Hall** (*33 Audubon Blvd., ℘504 865-5267 - www2.tulane.edu/calendar/arts.cfm*). It's free to peruse the fine art gallery at **The Newcomb Art Museum** (*Woldenberg Art Center, Newcomb Circle - ℘504 865 5328 - newcombartmuseum.tulane.edu - 10am-5pm; Sat. 11am-4pm; closed Sun and Mon*). The museum rotates exhibitions featuring pottery and ceramic works, contemporary painting, photography and other mediums from around the world.

Mid City and Bayou St. John★

Less than three miles north of the French Quarter, this largely residential neighborhood extends to Broad St., City Park, and Tulane and Esplanade Aves. on each side. Around Bayou St. John, you'll find the former sites of country homes for New Orleans' early wealthy citizens, when everything this far from the French Quarter was still swampland.
Areas of Mid City were devastated by Hurricane Katrina, and the neighborhood has spent the past decade in a process of rebuilding and rebirth, strengthening community and welcoming newcomers and change. In the commercial areas of Broad St., Canal St., Banks St. and Esplanade Ave., you'll find an energetic mix of legendary businesses, who held their ground during tribulations and change, and hip new inventions of young entrepreneurs that have popped up in the last few years.

▶**Access:** Streetcar lines: #47-Canal St.- Cemeteries and #48-Canal St.-City Park; Bus lines: #90 (Carrolton Ave.) and #91 (Esplanade Ave. to City Park).

Area map p. 50-51. Detachable map CE5-8.

▶**Tip:** From the CBD/French Quarter, two Canal St. streetcar lines end at City Park or the Lakeview Cemeteries, respectively, making it easy to plan which of those outings you'll choose first.

CITY PARK★★

DE6 *1 Palm Dr. (where N. Carrolton and Esplanade Aves. meet) - ℘504 482 4888 - www.neworleanscitypark.com.* Northwest of Jackson Square, this expansive urban park encompasses 1,300 acres at the head of gracious Esplanade Avenuea, which traces an old Choctaw path from the river to the Bayou St. John. Attractions include the New Orleans Botanical Garden, the just-for-kiddies Storyland and Carousel Gardens amusement parks, and City Putt, a kid (and adult!) -friendly mini golf course with New Orleans and Louisiana-themed holes. Developed recreational areas of the park include a series of paved walking paths, a lagoon with paddle boats for rent, golf course, frisbee golf course, and two stadiums. Many of the parks undeveloped corners and areas left to grow naturally, still represent the wild swampland once widespread to this area.

Paddling on Bayou St. John

NEW ORLEANS MUSEUM OF ART★

***E6** 1 Collins Diboll Cir. - ✆504 658-4100 - www.noma.org - Sat-Sun 10am-5pm; Tue-Fri 10am-6pm; Closed Mon. - $12, children under 12 $6.*
More than 40,000 pieces make up the permanent collection with works from major European and American schools of painting. Visiting exhibits and most of the permanent collection have a special focus on French works (Dégas, who visited New Orleans in 1870, Monet, Renoir, Pisarro and Gaugin are represented), Louisiana and African-American artists. You'll also find Japanese Edo-period paintings, a significant collection of pre-Columbian art, and several exquisite eggs by Russian jeweler Peter Carl Fabergé.

Adjacent to the museum, **The Sydney and Walda Besthoff Sculpture Garden** features more than 60 works by well known masters (Rodin, Oldenburg, Noguchi, Kohlmeyer and Moore, among others) artfully placed amid winding landscaped paths.

BAYOU ST. JOHN★★

***D6** Runs along Wisner Blvd. (adjacent to City Park, Moss St., and Jefferson Davis Parkway until Lafitte Ave.)*
Leave the Park from NOMA, crossing Carrollton Ave., and you'll land along the walking paths of Bayou St. John. This gorgeous urban waterway is the result of drained swampland between New Orleans and Lake Pontchartrain. Native Americans and early French explorers took to the waterways of the original Bayou St. John, which extended much farther, to explore the New Orleans and Mississippi River area.

Today, locals stroll along Bayou St. John and its bridges and picnic or take small boats to its waters. Several businesses (**Kayakitiyak** - *www.kayakitiyat.com*; **Bayou Paddlesports** - *www.bayoupaddlesports.com*) rent kayaks and lead tours along the Bayou.

Along the banks of Bayou St. John you'll find the **Pitot House**, a standing example of the early 19th-century country cottages that once prevailed in this area. This is only creole cottage of its kind that is also a museum, thanks to the Lousiana Landmark Society. (*1440 Moss St. - ✆504 482 0312 - www.louisianalandmarks.org/visit-pitot-house* - tours on the hour Wed.-Sun. 10am-3pm - $10)

THE LAFITTE GREENWAY

***E5** Along St Louis st. and Lafitte Ave., from Basin St. to N. Anthony St. - www.lafittegreenway.org .*
In 2015 the city finished the first stage of the Lafitte Greenway, a 2.6-mile trail and bikepath connecting the French Quarter to Mid City. Begin at the Basin St. entranceway, near Armstrong Park, and walk or bike the trail all the way to City Park. Along the way you'll pass through several New Orleans neighborhoods, with playgrounds, rec centers and greenery built up along the greenway.

LONG VUE HOUSE AND GARDENS★

***E5** 7 Bamboo Rd. - ☏504 488 5488 - www.longuevue.com - 10am-5pm, Sun 1pm-5pm - tours every hour -$12.*
On the way out of Mid City, of off Metairie Road and towards Lakeview and the Metairie suburbs, you'll find this historic house, garden and museum. The large, three-story house with a basement doesn't quite resemble the typical New Orleans shotgun house. Built instead during the "Country Place Era" over three years from 1939-1942, Longvue is one of the few houses representing this style of architecture. Tours of the main house showcase its fine architecture, American and English antiques, and a collection of fine art. The museum hosts a series of rotating art and culture exhibits. The vast gardens, built in 1935 by renowned female landscape architect Ellen Biddle Shipman, showcase dozens of species of magnolia, camellia, and citrus trees, as well as exotic flowers and plants.

CEMETERIES OF MID CITY AND BAYOU ST. JOHN

E6
Along Esplanade Ave., a few blocks before it meets with Bayou St. John, you'll find St. Louis Cemetery No.3 *(3421 Esplanade Ave. - ☏504 482 5065 - Mon.-Sat. 8am-4:30pm, Sun. 8am-4pm).*
This large cemetery was built in 1854. A piece of New Orleans history, tombs here indicate floods, yellow

New Orleans Museum of Art

fever outbreaks, and other population patterns and calamities in the city's history.

There are several prominent cemeteries in Mid City, all in the area where Canal St. meets with Canal Blvd., City Park Ave., and Metairie Rd. The largest is Greenwood Cemetery (120 City Park Ave.), the resting place of several mayors of New Orleans, Union and Confederate generals and soldiers. At the end of Canal Street, lies Charity Hospital Cemetery, the burial place for thousands who died at the hospital during a yellow fever outbreak in 1847. The Hurricane Katrina Memorial (5056 Canal St.) a solemn and respectful tribute to those who lost their lives during the storm, is built upon these grounds.

Treme★

Once referred to as the "back of town," this small, mostly residential neighborhood sits just above the French Quarter and is packed with its own culture and history.
The Faubourg Treme holds great historical significance as the city's first and primary neighborhood for free people of color. Over the decades, jazz musicians from Louis Prima to Kermit Ruffins called the Treme home.Treme is respected as a cradle of American music, and holds great importance in in African-American, creole and New Orleanian history and culture.

Detachable map AD4-6.
Tip: Combine a walk through the sights of the Treme with a trip to the nearby Faubourg Marigny. Both small neighborhoods can easily be toured in one day.

ARMSTRONG PARK AND CONGO SQUARE★

C4 *701 N Rampart St.; Armstrong Park is bound by St. Philip St., Rampart St., Basin St., St. Peter St., and N. Villere St.*
At the edge of Louis Armstrong Park, between Rampart and Basin streets, the cobblestoned area of **Congo Square** commemorates the place during French and Spanish colonial reign where slaves would gather on Sunday afternoons to trade crafts, socialize, drum, sing and dance. Many New Orleans musical and festival traditions (as well as American jazz, rhythm and blues) originated in large part because of these gatherings and the mix of cultural expressions that took place here.
Long before the arrival of European settlers, the Houmas Indians celebrated harvest season in this same sacred spot.
The rest of the park is dedicated to musical legends of New Orleans, and the history of jazz in the city. Throughout the year, the park holds many festivals, concerts, and free events.

Within Armstrong Park, just beyond Congo Square, the **Mahalia Jackson Theater for Performing Arts** (*1419 Basin St.*), named for the city's beloved gospel singer, hosts opera, ballet, and other live performances. Badly damaged by Hurricane Katrina in 2005, the 2,100-seat theater was renovated and reopened in 2009. (*www.mahaliajacksontheater.com*).

J&M RECORDING STUDIO

838 - 840 N. Rampart St.
A small plaque outside the door of a laundromat on the corner of N. Rampart and Dumaine Sts. clues music lover's in on the building's former fame. From 1945-1956, this

Mural in Treme

TREME
"From Congo Square, To Everywhere"

© Paul Broussard/New Orleans Convention and Visitors Bureau

St Augustine Church

building served as the J&M Recording Studio. The studio recorded such hits as Little Richard's *Tutti Frutti,* Fats Domino's *The Fat Man* and Professor Longhair's *Tipitina*. These hits and more of the small studio's late-1940s and '50s recordings were some of the first music dubbed Rock N' Roll. For this reason, many music historians and aficionados consider the studio as the birthplace of Rock N' Roll.

ST AUGUSTINE CHURCH★

C5 *1210 Governor Nicholls St. - ℘504 525 5934 - www.staugchurch.org.*
A donation from the Ursuline Sisters to the city's free people of color in 1841, this church is the oldest African American Catholic church in the United States. From its onset, the church and its organizations (including the Congregation of the Sisters of the Holy Family, the second-oldest African American congregation of women in the country) served to shelter and educate children of slaves, orphans, and the wider community. Today, the gorgeous church holds open mass on Sundays at 10am, with music from their gospel choir.
The Treme Fall Festival, a cultural event with food, music, and crafts, takes place here each year (*www. tremefest.com*).

JELLY ROLL MORTON'S HOUSE

B6 *1443 Frenchmen St.*
Early jazz hero Jelly Roll Morton was born and raised in this home on a residential section of Frenchmen St. Some credit him for inventing jazz, as Morton himself liked to brag, but all believe he was central in creating the genre as we know it. The house has since had other owners, and was renovated after Hurricane Katrina. Current residents often keep a picture of Jelly Roll Morton in the window of Creole Cottage.

ST. LOUIS CEMETERY NO.1★★

499 Basin St., between St. Louis and Conti Sts. - www.nolacatholiccemeteries.org.
One of the most popular ways to tour the above-ground graves of New Orleans historical fame is at this Treme cemetery, first laid out in late 1700s. Among the famous buried here: Marie Laveau, famed voodoo queen, Homer Plessy (of Plessy vs. Ferguson), and Etienne de Bure (the first mayor of New Orleans). The nonprofit group **Save Our Cemeteries** (*504 525 3377; www. saveourcemeteries.org*) leads tours from the Basin Street Station Visitors Center (*501 Basin St.*) Tours ($20) are frequent and easy to join. You must be part of a tour to enter the cemetery).

© Louisiana Office of Tourism

St. Louis Cemetery No.1

BACKSTREET CULTURAL MUSEUM★

B4-5 *1116 Henriette Delille St. - 504 577 6001 - Tues-Sat 10am-4pm; Closed Sun. and Mon - www. backstreetmuseum.org - $10.*
Dominiq Francis's small, friendly museum displays the most fantastic costumes of Mardi Gras indians over the years. A stop at Francis's house in Treme is an excellent way to gain local, insider knowledge of some of the most fascinating and rich traditions in New Orleans' Mardi Gras culture.

Faubourg Marigny

Referred to often as just "The Marigny" (*faubourg *is French for "suburb"), this triangle-shaped area touches the French Quarter at Esplanade Ave. and extends to Franklin Ave. downriver, between Rampart St. and the Mississippi. The neighborhood was laid out in the early part of the 19th Century by a Creole developer named Brenard de Marigny. Today, it's home to a notorious music scene, in the streets and clubs around Frenchmen Street. The neighborhood is known for colorful houses, eclectic shops and cafes, live music, and historic mansions along Esplanade Ave.

▶**Access:** Streetcar lines: #49 Rampart-St. Claude; Bus lines: #55 (Elysian Fields Ave.); #5 (Decatur/N.Peters Sts.).

Detachable map AC3-4.

▶**Tip:** Experience the Marigny in the evening or night, when the music and people of the area really come to life.

FRENCHMEN STREET★★

***A4** 400-600 Frenchmen street, Faubourg Marigny.*

Tourists in search of the "real" nightlife of New Orleans depart Bourbon St. and wander ten blocks upriver to the 400-600 blocks of Frenchmen Street, where perhaps the highest concentration of live music in the city abounds. Any night of the week you'll see amateur bands performing on street corners for crowds of onlookers, and the sound of brass bands, jazz and contemporary local music can be heard wafting out of every door. Many clubs have early sets on weekend afternoons, but things really get started after dark and, on weekends, continue well until dawn.

CRESCENT PARK

***B4** Entrances to the park only on Piety St. in the Bywater and Marigny St. in Faubourg Marigny - 6am-7:30pm.*

Plans for this urban greenway began with the hope to extend the downtown river boardwalk from the French Quarter all the way to the 9th Ward. While this isn't quite complete, this landscaped greenway and walking path is a beautiful way to view the Mississippi River and surrounding areas. The current park extends 20 acres and 1.4 miles, with bike paths, riverside pavilions and rest areas decorated with plants, flowers and sculpture.

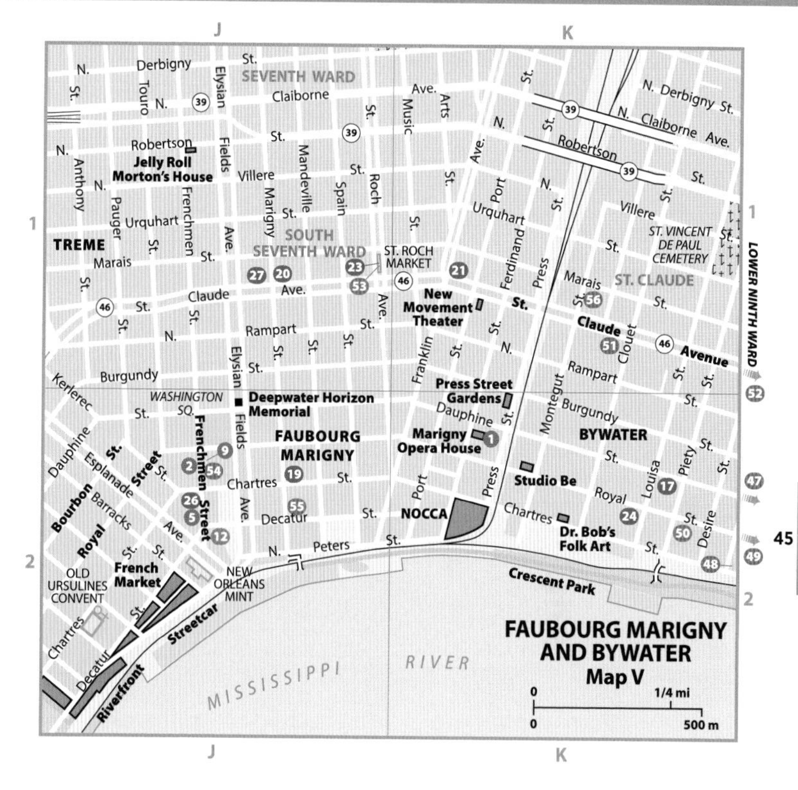

DEEPWATER HORIZON MEMORIAL★

A4 *2201 Dauphine St.*
A circle of eleven life-sized steel figures stands at a busy intersection of the Marigny, memorializing the men who died during an explosion at BP's Deepwater Horizon oil drilling facility.

The artist Jason Kimes uses a pointillism technique to construct the 500-pound sculptures out of small discs. The project was conceptualized by Michael Manjarris, co-founder of the non-profit Sculpture for New Orleans, after Manjarris sat next to a father of one of the victims on an airplane and was deeply affected by his story.

© Paul Broussard/New Orleans Convention and Visitors Bureau

Musicians on Frenchmen Street

MARIGNY OPERA HOUSE

725 St Ferdinand St. - ☏504 948 9998 - www.marignyoperahouse.org.
This gorgeous stone building was first erected in 1853 by architect Theodore Giraud and served as a Catholic Church for German residents of Faubourg Marigny. Decades later, the Marigny Opera House utilizes the excellent acoustics for a diverse calendar of performances, forming what they call a "church of the arts." With intricately tiled floors, archways, and original hanging lanterns, it's worth attending one of the house's performances for a peek inside this architectural gem.

NEW ORLEANS CENTER FOR CREATIVE ARTS (NOCCA)

2800 Chartres St. - ☏504 940 2787 - www.nocca.org
Since 1973, NOCCA has been providing professional arts education to secondary school students. Graduates of NOCCA over the include contemporary music legends like Harry Connick Jr., Trombone Shorty, Jonathan Batiste, the Marsalis' Brothers, actor Wendell Pierce and NPR radio personality Poppy Tooker. The school often hosts performances, and showcases student work within the red-bricked building at the **Kirschman Gallery**.

Bywater

Muraled warehouses, colorful shotguns, and artistic communities make up the bywater neighborhood, from the train tracks at Press Street to the industrial canal on the other side, and bordered by the commercial throughway of St. Claude avenue amd the mississippi river.

▶**Access: Streetcar line:** #49 Rampart-St.Claude; Bus lines: #88 (Rampart St./St. Claude Ave and #5 (Decatur/Chartres Sts.).

Detachable map AC3-4.

▶**Tip:** There are fewer big-ticket tourist sights in Bywater, but with its artists' studios, delicious cafes and entertaining nightlife on St. Claude Ave, it's the perfect way to spend a relaxed, alternative day of your trip.

STUDIO BE★★

B4 *2941 Royal St. - ☎504 330-6231 - www.brandanodums.com/project/studio-be - Weds.-Sat. 2-8pm.*
Marked by one of the most photographed, brightly-colored murals in the neighborhood, this large warehouse is home to the artwork of Brandan Odums, a visual artist and filmmaker known for his street art and public projects touching on themes of racism, social injustice, and issues in the South. Odum's first solo exhibit, here his larger-than-life murals fill the rooms of a 35,000 square foot warehouse and make for an impactful afternoon of contemporary art.

DR. BOB'S FOLK ART

3027 Chartres St. - ☎504 945 2225 - www.drbobart.net. Famous for such phrases like "Be Nice or Leave," Dr. Bob's colorful, painted signs are an iconic part of New Orleans folk art. A wide collection of his whimsical work is available here for viewing and purchase.

ST. CLAUDE AVENUE

This busy avenue extends from the Marigny to the Industrial Canal and is home to a hip, eclectic mix of galleries, performance venues, restaurants, bars and music clubs.

PRESS STREET GARDENS

7 Press St - ☎504 940 2808 - www.pressstreetgardens.com -
The verdant urban farm and gardens, just off of the Press St. train tracks, is operated by the NOCCA Institute. It serves as a learning center for NOCCA students and the wider Bywater-Marigny community, where residents can learn about sustainable methods of growing food and plants.

The Lower Ninth Ward

Few areas of New Orleans were hit as hard by Hurricane Katrina as the Lower Ninth Ward, a lower income neighborhood devastated by the storm and given much attention by national media. Today, the neighborhood's residents are dedicated to celebrating the binds of community and bright future ahead for the neighborhood, while honoring its storied history. The Lower 9 is across the Industrial Canal from the Bywater and reachable by bridges at St. Claude, Claiborne, and Florida Aves.

▶**Access:** Bus lines: #88 (St. Claude Ave.), #84 (Claiborne Ave).
Detachable map AC3-4.
▶**Tip:** Because this neighborhood experiences a higher level of crime than others and can be reached only by bridges, it's best to move around here by car, cab or bus.

THE HOUSE OF DANCE AND FEATHERS★★

B4 *1317 Tupelo St. - ✆504 957 2678 - www.houseofdanceandfeathers.org - visits by appt. only - free, donations welcome.* This small, personal museum celebrates the gorgeous traditions of Mardi Gras far from the more commercialized images of Bourbon Street partiers or huge-float parades.

Among the groups immortalized in Ronald W. Lewis's museum are the Mardi Gras Indians, close-knit African American groups whose festive traditions are rooted in African and Native American culture, but have evolved into their own cultural expressions over the years. Come springtime, Mardi Gras Indians dance, beat drums, and don flamboyantly feathered, and intricately beaded costumes.

Another feature here are The Social Aid and Pleasure Clubs, citizens of New Orleans responsible for the second line funerals, honoring the dead only as this city could; and the Skull and Bones, spooky and mysterious krewes dressed as skeletons to honor the dead. Visits are by appointment only (the museum is in Ronald's home), and admission is donation-based.

THE LOWER NINTH WARD LIVING MUSEUM★★

1235 Deslonde St. - ✆504 220 3652 - www.l9livingmuseum.org - 12-5pm; closed Mondays - free, donations welcome.

Through exhibits and oral storytelling, The Lower 9th Ward Living Museum tells the story of a neighborhood with a long, rich history, highlighting the firsthand experiences of

The House of Dance and Feathers

community members. The museum's collection traces cultural and historically-significant events in the neighborhood bot long, long before Katrina and in the decade after the storm.

FATS DOMINO'S HOUSE

1208 Caffin Ave.
When touring the neighborhood, don't forget to stop by Fats Domino's House and pay tribute to the recently departed musical legend. The neighborhood honors that Fats, a hugely successful musician in the 50s and 60s, still chose to return to his Lower Ninth Ward home on breaks from tour.

Unlike the home's of many music legends around the city, which have no markers and new residents, Domino's house is impossible to miss. It's painted bright yellow with black trim, and FD's initials are emblazoned across the front.

DOULLUT STEAMBOAT HOUSES

400 and 503 Egania Sts.
Along the Holy Cross levee, marvel at the fascinatingly bizarre architecture of the Doullout Steamboat Houses, 1900s houses built by a steamboat river captain and his son, and meant to resemble the ships. (Both Domino's house and the steamboat houses are private residences that you can view only from the outside).

Day Trips from New Orleans

From swamplands to quaint, small towns, there are many reasons to venture out of the immediate New Orleans area and explore. Across Lake Pontchartrain, the North Shore is a largerly suburban area that still contains some of its original swamps, bayous, woods and wildlife. In the areas to the east of New Orleans and on the West Bank of the Mississippi River, Vietnamese and other immigrant populations flourish. Some of the best shrimp and fresh Gulf seafood can be found here.

▶**Access:** The North shore is best accessed by car. The Algiers/Canal Street Ferry, #100, #101 and #108 reach the West Bank neighborhoods of Algiers and Gretna. New Orleans East can be reached by the #64 bus, but the East and Chalmette are most easily explored by car.

Detachable map AD1-4.

▶**Tip:** The Causeway, the bridge connecting New Orleans and the Northshore, becomes dangerous (and often closes) during fog and bad weather.

THE NORTH SHORE

CD4

Most towns on the Northshore are reachable via The Lake Pontchartrain Causeway, a bridge connecting Metairie, Louisiana, just north of New Orleans, with Mandeville, La across the lake. The Causeway in itself is an incredible sight to witness: at 23.83 miles it is the longest bridge over continuous water in the world. The long bridge spans over a the flat, calm waters of Lake Pontchartrain, an oval-shaped, shallow (12-14 ft. deep) estuary made up of brackish water.

Fontainebleau State Park★

62883 Hwy. 1089, Mandeville, LA - ✆985-624-4443 - www.crt.state.la.us - day access 6am-9pm (10pm Fri and Sat) - $3. In the 1800s, this land along the shore of Lake Pontchartrain supported a sugar plantation owned by the wealthy Bernard de Marigny de Mandeville.

Today, its a 2,800-acre park celebrating the Louisiana wetlands and their diverse species. The park includes a beach, nature trails, and lakeside cabins for rent. Fontainebleau is surrounded by water (Lake Pontchartrain, Bayou Cane and Bayou Castine) on each side.

Running through the park is the **Tammany Trace** (*www.tammanytrace.org*), a former railroad line converted to a paved walking and biking path. The 31-mile trace connects much of

© Louisiana Office of Tourism/Tim Mueller Photography

Fontainebleau State Park

the North Shore and allows bikers to explore the towns of Mandeville, Covington, Abita Springs, Lacombe and Slidell.

Abita Brewery

21084 LA-36, Covington, LA - ✆504 893 3143 -www.abita.com. The first craft brewery in the New Orleans area has over the years expanded to national fame. Accessible by the Tammany Trace bike trail, the brewery, with its comfotable tap room serving casual pub fare, is a great place for a rest stop. Tours run every half hour.

Abita Mystery House

22275 LA-36, Abita Springs, LA - ✆985 892-2624 -www.abitamystery house.com - daily 10am-5pm - $3. Near the brewery in the town of Abita Springs is this quirky museum. Walls of broken glass, dozens of old telephones, pinball machines, and an entire house of hot sauce bottles: this is an eclectic, special place. The small, rambling structures here feature layers and layers of kitschy collections and oddball rarities. A passion project of its owners, visitors will often run into the museum's patron as he makes small repairs to his vast collection.

THE WEST BANK

Across the river from downtown New Orleans; accessible via the Algiers Point Ferry or the Crescent City Connection Bridge.

© Zack Smith Photography/New Orleans Convention and Visitors Bureau

Houses in Algiers Point

Algiers Point★

The second oldest neighborhood in New Orleans, "The Point" lies directly across the river from the French Quarter. Step off the ferry and onto the levee path, a bike and walking path that stretches along the river. A series of plaques along the levee path note the neighborhood's storied past in relation to the city of New Orleans. As early as 1719, the swamplands of Algiers were cleared out for plantation space by early French (and later Spanish) settlers. Later, it became home to slave barracks, where slaves were held before being ferried over the river for sale in the French Market. At other times, Algiers was home to the city's powder magazine, where gunpowder was stored, and later the slaughterhouses.

Today it's a small residential neighborhood, easily accessible from New Orleans by a short ferry ride leaving from the bottom of Canal Street, or by car on **the Crescent City Connection**, crossing the Mississippi River. With its blooming Japanese magnolia trees, cobblestone streets, ornate shotguns and gas-lit porch lamps it shares much in character with the French Quarter.

Take a walk through the charming neighborhood with its coffee shops and small business, and visit **The Cita Dennis Hubbell Branch** of New Orleans Public Library, settled in 1907 and the oldest library in the city. The beautiful Romanesque **Algiers Courthouse**, directly across from the river, was built in 1896 to replace a plantation home that served as the courthouse until it was destroyed in a fire.

Gretna

5 miles southeast of downtown New Orleans via US I-90.

Every Saturday morning, local bakers, cooks, farmers and fisherman flock to the small town square in downtown Gretna, Louisiana, a riverside town on the West Bank of the Mississippi. The Saturday Gretna Farmers' Market is an excellent way to try every local specialty, from boudin to fresh crabs, and vegetables grown just up the road. In the fall, Gretna throws a free music festival featuring local brass, Cajun and zydeco bands as well as big headliners like KISS, Huey Lewis and the News, and Pat Benatar. During Gretna Festival, a ferry runs from Canal Street in New Orleans' CBD to downtown Gretna (the ferry was once in regular operation, but now only runs for special occasions).

Vietnamese Communities

Seeking refuge during the Vietnam War (in Vietnam, the American War), many Vietnamese families found a new home in New Orleans, with the Catholic working to help ease the transition. Today, Vietnamese communities are a vibrant, essential part of New Orleans' diverse cultural landscape. Many settled in New Orleans East and on the West Bank, in communities like Gretna, and so the West Bank has some of the city's best Vietnamese food. In New Orleans East, at the time of Vietnamese New Year (Jan. or Feb. according to lunar calendar), the local archdiocese throws a spectacular festival with food, live music (traditional Vietnamese and contemporary New Orleans), fireworks and games.
A trip from New Orleans across the river is well worth it to eat some of the most delicious Vietnamese food in the central United States. Restaurants Tan Dinh, Nine Roses and Pho Bang are excellent choices authentic bowls of pho, banh mi, and noodle and rice specialties.

Hong Kong Food Market

925 Behrman Hwy #3, Gretna - ℘504 394 7075 - 7:30am-9pm. A vast market serving the West Bank's Asian communities, this shop has an impressive and diverse collection of imported goods. The selection of noodles, spices, dried seafood and Southeast Asian fruit and vegetables are a delight for foodies.

Barrataria Preserve★

6588 Barataria Blvd. in Marrero, 17mi south of New Orleans near Crown Point.Take US-90 West over the Mississippi River; exit at Barataria Blvd. and go south on Rte. 45 to park. ℘504-689-3690 or 504-589-2133 - www.nps.gov/jela. This 23,000-acre wetland wilderness characterizes the constantly shifting terrain of the Mississippi delta region. Ranger-led hikes and guided canoe trips unlock the mysteries of this unique environment, as do exhibits in the preserve's visitor center.
An adventurous way to see the Bayou Barataria up close is to take one of several privately operated swamp tours

CHALMETTE BATTLEFIELD★

AB2-3 *5mi southeast of New Orleans in Chalmette. Go east on Rte. 46 to park entrance at 8606 W. St. Bernard Hwy. ℘504-281-0510 or 504-589-2133. www.nps.gov/jela*
At this riverside battlefield on January 8, 1815, Gen. Andrew Jackson and a force of about 5,000 soldiers successfully defended New Orleans against British invasion in the final major confrontation of the War of 1812, thus securing US ownership of the Louisiana Territory.
In the visitor center, displays and interactive exhibits recount the battle.

Whitney Plantation

Afterward, you can drive or walk the 1.5mi road leading past key battle sites, and visit the peaceful National Cemetery.

WHITNEY PLANTATION★★

C1-2 I

5099 Louisiana Hwy 18, Edgard, LA - ℘225 265 3300 - whitneyplantation.com - 9:30am-5pm; closed Tuesdays.
This incredibly moving, somber museum is the only plantation home in the area that has been dedicated to the lives of slaves. The museum contains impeccably maintained properties from the original plantation, from the Creole Cottage "big house" to a blacksmith's shop, Baptist church, and two former slave quarter houses. Art, photography, sculpture and several monuments — one emblazoned with over 100,000 known names of former slaves—honor slaves and their children. Plantation visits are lead by a tour guide. Whether touring the home alone or in conjunction with other plantations in the area, visiting the Whitney Plantation provides a more truthful representation of plantation life as it was for everyone involved.

Overnight Trips: Cajun Country

A broad landscape of sugarcane and rice fields, boggy swamps and sinuous bayous, Cajun Country offers visitors an excellent opportunity to sample the rich cultural heritage of one of the nation's best-known ethnic groups.

▶**Access:** From New Orleans, take I-10 West toward Baton Rouge to explore the area around Lafayette and the Atchafalaya Basin, about 130 miles from downtown New Orleans .

Area map p. 83. Detachable map DF3-4.

▶**Tips:** Plan to spend as much time in the small towns of the surrounding area as in Lafayette itself. See *www.louisianatravel.com* or www.*cajuncountry.org*.

CAJUN COUNTRY★★

Comprising 22 parishes (the Louisiana term for counties), the region extends north of the ragged Gulf Coast and west of the Mississippi River, encompassing the boggy Atchafalaya Basin and relatively high prairies ranging west of Lafayette to the Texas border. Formally nicknamed "Acadiana," the Cajun Country is principally inhabited by descendants of French colonists who were deported from Acadia (now Nova Scotia, Canada) in 1755 for refusing to swear allegiance to the British Crown. After suffering terrible hardships, Acadian refugees began arriving in southern Louisiana in the late 18C, infusing the region with the distinctive culture that flourishes today. Tourist attractions are widely scattered outside the regional capital of Lafayette, but the charm of a visit to this area lies in its people and their lifestyle.

Explore the small towns of St. Martinville, Breaux Bridge or Opelousas, where fun-loving, hardworking and fervently Catholic Cajuns welcome visitors to join their enthusiastic pursuit of a good time. Fiddles and accordions set feet flying in rural dance halls; headily spiced gumbos, seafood stews and boudin (rice and pork sausage) appear on local tables; and Cajun French is as prevalent as English on the sidewalks.

LAFAYETTE★

D3 *135mi west of New Orleans via I-10. Visitor center at 1400 N.W. Evangeline Thruway. ℘800-346-1958.*

Founded in 1836 as Vermilionville and renamed in 1884, Louisiana's fourth-largest city is known as the "Hub City

© Ian Dagnall/age fotostock

Cathedral of Saint John the Evangelist, Lafayette

of Acadiana". Several Acadian-related sights lie within its boundaries, and its many hotels and restaurants make it a natural headquarters for explorations of the surrounding region.

ACADIAN CULTURAL CENTER★★

501 Fisher Road, Lafayette - ✆337-232-0789

This well-conceived visitor center operated by the Jean Lafitte National Historical Park and Preserve is an ideal place to begin forays into the Cajun Country. Displays focus on various aspects of Cajun life in Louisiana, highlighting the ways in which Acadian traditions and methods—farming and building techniques, clothing, language, crafts, music—were adapted to conditions in the new land. A 40min video dramatizes the Acadian expulsion from Nova Scotia.

Music on the Bayou

In Cajun Country, the fun begins when the day's work is done, and for many Cajuns fun means heading to local stages or dance halls to step, swing and stomp to the pulse-quickening sounds of Cajun and zydeco music. Typical Cajun bands incorporate accordions, fiddles and guitars along with bass and percussion (including washboards and tambourines), all accompanying a lead singer warbling in French about ill-fated love, family relationships and the joys of eating, drinking, dancing and living life to the fullest. In the course of its evolution from its roots in Acadian folk music, Cajun music has been much influenced by African, country and bluegrass musical traditions. Today it is enjoying a resurgence thanks to star performers such as Michael Doucet and his band BeauSoleil. Also accordion-based, zydeco music developed in the mid-20C on the prairies of southeastern Louisiana at the hands of such pioneers as Clifton Chenier and Boozoo Chavis, who applied rhythm-and-blues elements to traditional Creole music forms. Soul, disco and reggae music continue to exert an influence on zydeco, and a profusion of zydeco dance halls attests to its growing popularity.

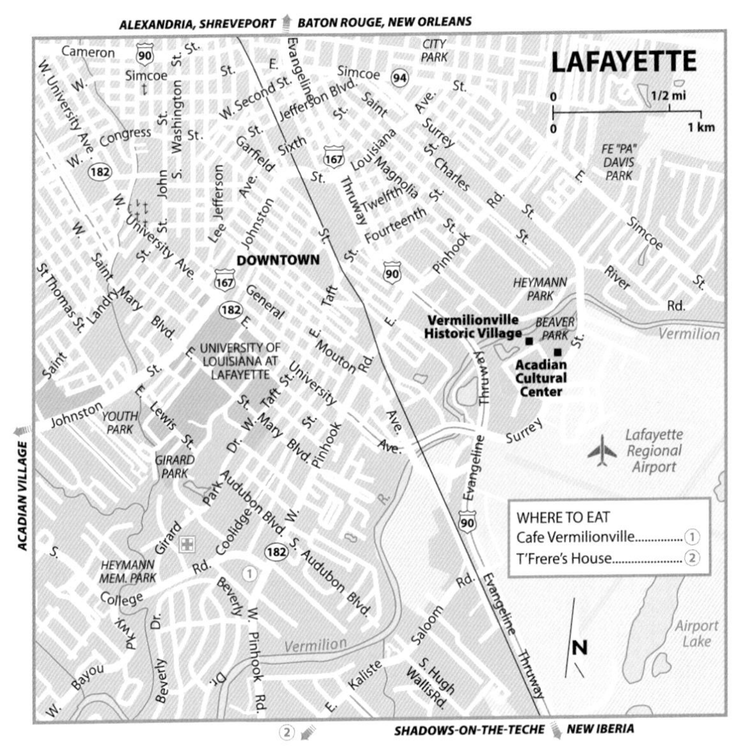

In spring and fall, the center operates guided boat tours on languid Bayou Vermilion, former home to trappers, farmers and fishermen; it's a great way to get a feel for the traditional Cajun lifestyle of yesteryear.

VERMILIONVILLE★

D3 *M° Madeleine 300 Fisher Rd. ✆337 233-4077. www.vermilionville.org.* Eighteen colorfully recreated and restored buildings, including a 1790 farmstead, range along tranquil Bayou Vermilion at this living-history museum and folklife park devoted to commemorating the Acadian

Shadows on the Teche

way of life between 1765 and 1890. Costumed artisans demonstrate traditional crafts such as weaving, boatbuilding and blacksmithing, while Cajun bands perform regularly in a large performance hall. Don't miss a browse through the gift shop for locally-produced handicrafts.

ACADIAN VILLAGE★★

E4 *M° 200 Greenleaf Dr. ℘337-981-2364. www.acadianvillage.org.*
Set around a placid "bayou," this rustic re-created village offers a glimpse of life in Acadiana around the mid-19C. Most of the structures are originals, moved here from other locations in the region; others were constructed on-site with period materials. Helpful plaques provide insights into architectural practices of the time, while displays in each building focus on Acadian culture and traditions.harmonious contrast with the 19C colonnades of the courtyard garden, though its addition was controversial at the time.
Today the arcades house old-fashioned shops, elegant designer fashion boutiques and art galleries and the Palais-Royal has become a hip hotspot for fashionistas.
Perhaps the most charming element of this area is the network of little passageways that surround the galleries.

SHADOWS ON THE TECHE ★★

***E4** 317 E. Main St., New Iberia. zVisit by guided tour only. ℘337-369-6446. www.shadowsontheteche.org*
Vivienne (1823), lit Moss-draped live oak trees create a play of light and shadow over this elegant brick Greek Revival mansion, built by sugarcane planter David Weeks in 1834. Distinguished by its dignified columned facade, the house remained in the Weeks family for four generations before being left to the National Trust for Historic Preservation.
You'll feel you've traveled back in time on a visit here, as nearly every item in the house is original, including fine Federal and Empire-style furniture from New York and Philadelphia, Staffordshire china and family portraits.
Family members lie interred in a tranquil corner of the formally landscaped grounds fringing the slow-moving Bayou Teche.
Guided tours are offered daily, as well as a lively schedule of activities, from Halloween events in the gardens to arts and crafts fairs.

STAY, EAT AND DRINK IN CAJUN COUNTRY★

Cafe Vermilionville – *1304 W. Pinhook, Lafayette - ℘337-237-0100. www.cafev.com - Louisiana French.* Site of Vermilionville's first inn back in the early 1800s, this cafe in Lafayette's Oil Center now houses one of Lafayette's finest restaurants. The unvarnished wooden beams, hanging plants and candlelight blend romance with country elegance (jackets required). Raveworthy specialties include jumbo shrimp in a spicy herb sauce, crawfish beignets and pan-seared amberjack.

Jolie's Louisiana Bistro – *507 W. Pinhook Rd., Lafayette - ℘337-504-2382 - www.jolieslouisianabistro.com - Creole.* This unfussy bistro melds traditional Creole cooking with a farm-to-table philosophy, serving delicious steaks and local seafood creations such as the Zapp's Crawtator-Crusted Louisiana drumfish. The charcuterie and cheese boards are both winners.

E4 **T'Frere's House** – *1905 Verot School Rd., Lafayette - ℘337-984-9347 or 800-984-9347 - www.tfrereshouse.com- 8 rooms.* You'll be immersed in Acadiana at this traditional bayou mansion on the edge of town. Antiques from the 18C and 19C take you back to 1880, when it was built. Guests particularly enjoy the ritual daily "Twilight Time" gatherings complete with juleps and crab canapés. The huge Cajun breakfast is the highlight: eggs, spicy smoked sausage, and crepes topped with sugar-cane syrup.

Overnight Trips: Gulf Coast

Long a popular resort haven, the coastline fringing the Gulf of Mexico from Mobile, Alabama, to New Orleans, Louisiana, boasts a wide variety of attractions for gamblers, sportsmen and history buffs, as well as those seeking the pleasures of sun and sand.

Access: 225-635-0090; www.louisianatravel.com; 228-896-6699, www.gulfcoast.org; (Biloxi); 251-208-2000, www.mobile.org (Mobile).
Parking: Long distances between resort towns make driving essential here. During the winter, parking lots will be full of cars with license plates from northern states.

Area map p. 88-89. Detachable map E1.

HISTORY OF THE GULF COAST

Claimed by the French government in the late 17C, this area came under British rule in 1763 following French defeat in the French and Indian War, and was ceded to Spain following the American Revolution. The American flag was first raised over the territory in 1811, and resort communities sprang up. Staunchly Confederate through the Civil War, the Gulf Coast fell to Union forces in 1864.

In the years following Reconstruction, tourism again boomed in the area. Hurricane Katrina devastated much of this area in 2005; recovery efforts were ongoing in April 2010 when an explosion occurred at the Deepwater Horizon oil drilling platform offshore, sending the entire rig to the bottom and leaving the oil well at the seafloor uncapped. Before the well was sealed, an estimated 4.9 million barrels of oil gushed into the Gulf, slicking waterways, beaches and wetlands all along the Louisiana, Mississippi and Alabama shores with raw crude. The environmental and economic damage of the disaster are still being calculated. Tourism at the resort communities of Gulf Shores, Pascagoula, Biloxi, Ocean Springs and Gulfport slowed in the aftermath of the disaster but today, after successful cleanup efforts, these cities are again attracting visitors to their white-sand beaches, warm gulf waters and moderate year-round temperatures, although some historic structures were lost.

Biloxi Bay Bridge viewed from Ocean Springs Beach

BILOXI

90 miles northeast of New Orleans on US I-10.

This bustling coastal Mississippi city teems with activity from its resorts, fishing port, seafood canneries and boatyards, all blessings of its waterbound location on a peninsula between Biloxi Bay and the Mississippi Sound. Founded in 1699, Biloxi was accessible only by steamboat during the antebellum period; it nevertheless became one of the most popular resorts on the Gulf Coast.

Biloxi was hard hit by Hurricane Katrina in 2005; the massive storm came ashore just west of the city and flooded the entire shorefront area, bringing water into beachfront hotels and washing barge-based casinos inland.

Today both new and rebuilt casinos dot the miles of beach along Biloxi's shorefront. Katrina's winds and tidal surge wiped away the charming homes that used to line the residential stretches of Beach Boulevard. Continuing to rebuild from that devastating event, the city welcomes thousands each May to the popular Biloxi Shrimp Festival.

OCEAN SPRINGS★

1mi east of Biloxi via US-90.

This waterside artists' colony in Mississippi invites strolls along pleasant sidewalks lined with antique

Dauphin Street, Mobile

shops, studios, art galleries and cafes. Also in town is the **William M. Colmer Visitor Center** (*3500 Park Rd., off US-90; 228-230-4100; www.nps.gov/guis*) of the Gulf Islands National Seashore, a national park that preserves the Gulf Coast barrier islands.

OHR-O'KEEFE MUSEUM OF ART

386 Beach Blvd., Biloxi. 228- 374-5547 - www.georgeohr.org - daily. Tues-Sat 10am-5pm - closed Sun and Mon - $10.

Starchitect Frank Gehry designed this stunning museum, surrounded by towering live oak trees. The museum is a temple potter George Ohr (the O'Keefe is not Georgia O'Keefe but the museum's patron, Jeremiah "Jerry" O'Keefe. George Ohr (1857-1918) called himself the "Mad Potter of Biloxi" and is considered an early leader in the modernist ceramics movement. During his life, his work was considered radical, defying the aesthetic conventions of the time, and so even today, a century after his death, his work continues to appear contemporary. The museum holds regular exhibitions of avant-garde works—paintings, installations, drawings, sculptures, and pottery—as well as fun ceramics classes.

MOBILE

A1 *On Mobile Bay, 62 miles northeast of Biloxi on US I-10.*

The third-largest city in Alabama, this gracious port combines the

genteel atmosphere of the antebellum era with the bustle and verve of a contemporary southern metropolis. Mobile served as the capital of French Louisiana from 1711 to 1719. Its prime location at the head of Mobile Bay made the city a major Confederate port during the Civil War, one of the last to fall to Union control.
Today the Port of Mobile and shipbuilding activities at the Alabama Shipyards fuel Mobile's economy. The city prides itself on its French heritage; the Mardi Gras celebration here predates the better-known festivities in New Orleans and signals the start of the dazzling annual Azalea Trail Festival. Local maps and information are available at the visitor center downtown in **Fort Condé** *(150 S. Royal St.; ℘251-208-7508; www.museumofmobile.com)*, a reconstructed version of the early-18C French outpost. Mobile's population exploded in the last decade as people moved from New Orleans in the wake of Hurricane Katrina.

USS Alabama Battleship Memorial Park

2703 Battleship Pkwy., off US-90 1mi east of downtown. ℘251 433 2703. www.ussalabama.com. Launched in 1942, this massive ship served in both the Atlantic and Pacific theaters of World War II, and earned nine battle stars shooting down 22 enemy planes and participating in six land bombardments.
The self-guided tour offers a rare opportunity to enter a massive barbette supporting one of the ship's 16-inch gun turrets. Other attractions in the park include the World War II submarine USS Drum, and 27 historic aircraft.

Museum of Mobile

111 S. Royal St. - ℘251-208-7508. www.museumofmobile.com.
An extensive and varied collection of documents, portraits, Civil War artifacts, and Mardi Gras memorabilia housed in Mobile's historic market building tells the story of Mobile from colonization to the present. Exhibits change frequently; there's also a fun hands-on Discovery Room for kids.

Gulf Coast Exploreum Museum of Science★

65 Government St. at Water St. ℘251-208-6893. www.exploreum.com.
Sleek and sparkling, the Exploreum features interactive exhibits that encourage kids to get excited about physics. In Hands-On Hall, more than 50 interactive physics displays entertain and educate visitors. Visitors can conduct a variety of biologically oriented experiments in BioLab, in-vestigate the workings of the human body in BodyWorks, and explore the world of chemistry in ChemLab.

Bellingrath Home and Gardens

20mi south of Mobile via I-10 to US-90. 12401 Bellingrath Rd., Theodore, AL.- ℘251 973 2217. Begun in 1927, some 65 acres of beautifully landscaped gardens surround this Mediterranean-style villa (1935) of antique brick and ironwork. Mobile soft-drink magnate Walter Bellingrath and his wife created this exquisite haven on the

© Meinzahn/iStockphoto.com

Bellingrath Home and Gardens

bank of the Fowl River as a personal retreat, decorating the house with Mrs. Bellingrath's extensive collection of European antique furniture, china and porcelain. The rose garden ranks among the finest in the country; you can also stroll a Bayou Boardwalk.

WHERE TO EAT AND STAY IN GULF COAST

The Shed Barbecue and Blues Joint
7501 MS-57, Ocean Springs, MS - ☏228 875 9590 - www.theshedbbq.com - 10:30am-9pm. On your way from New Orleans to the coast, make a stop at the Shed, some of the best barbecue in the region. The rambling shack of a restaurant is decorated in entertaining signage and license plates, with several wide porches and covered areas for dining. Live blues and local rock music perform here almost nightly.

Aunt Jenny's Catfish Restaurant
1217 Washington Ave, Ocean Springs, MS - ☏228 875 9201- www.auntjennyscatfish.com - Mon-Wed. 4pm-9pm; Thu-Sun. 11am-9pm. This friendly restaurant serves large, delicious platters of southern fried catfish and chicken. The dining room looks out onto a picturesque small bayou. The welcoming staff are more than ready take you on a tour and tell you the history of the building: first a sacred Indian ground, then a plantation house, and later a hospital-run health resort (the water near the restaurant was thought to have healing properties). The restaurant has a basement, speakeasy-like bar, with a corner booth (unfortunately the original was destroyed by flooding) where Elvis is known to have spent some late evenings.

Admiral Hotel Mobile
251 Government Street,Mobile, Alabama - ☏251 432 8000 - www.curiocollection3.hilton.com, wifi and breakfast not included. $99-175. This small, refined hotel in a historic downtown building, is walking distance to the Gulf Coast Exploreum Science Center, the History Museum of Mobile, the Alabama Contemporary Art Center, as well as many shops and restaurants. Rooms are standard but comfortable, with nice views of downtown Mobile. An outdoor swimming pool includes cabanas.

Overnight Trips: River Road★

One of the finest collections of antebellum plantation houses inthe South lies along the historic River Road between New Orleans and Baton Rouge, Louisiana. Lined with more than 2,000 plantations in its early-19C heyday, these banks of the Mississippi have since been marred by a glut of 20C oil and chemical plants.

▶**Access:** The River Road traces both banks of the Mississippi for approximately 120mi between New Orleans and Baton Rouge. More information: *℘225-635-0090; www.louisianatravel.com.*

Area map p. 96. Detachable map G1-3.

HISTORY OF RIVER ROAD

G1-3

Beginning in the early 18C, Louisiana's French colonial government encouraged agricultural development of this area by granting plots of land to individuals who established plantations. Cotton, indigo, rice and especially sugarcane all thrived in the rich soil of the Mississippi River flood-plain, providing planters with the means to live extravagantly.

Large homes built by slave labor formed the heart of most plantations; the principal entryway faced the river. After 1803, Greek Revival became the popular style, and many Creole-style homes were updated with Classical ornamentation.

Madewood (1846), designed by noted Louisiana architect Henry Howard, is considered among the finest examples of Greek Revival architecture in the area *(4250 Hwy. 308, 2mi south of Napoleonville; ℘985-369-7151; www.madewood.com)*.

The term "River Road" designates roadways on both sides of the river and incorporates sections of several state highways (notably Highway 18 on the west bank, and Highway 44 on the east bank). Route numbers change along the way; it's best to keep to the levees.

The Hale Boggs Bridge *(I-310)*, **the Veterans Memorial Bridge** *(Hwy. 641)* and the **Sunshine Bridge** *(Hwy. 70)* allow access between the east and west banks.

The following sights are organized from south to north.

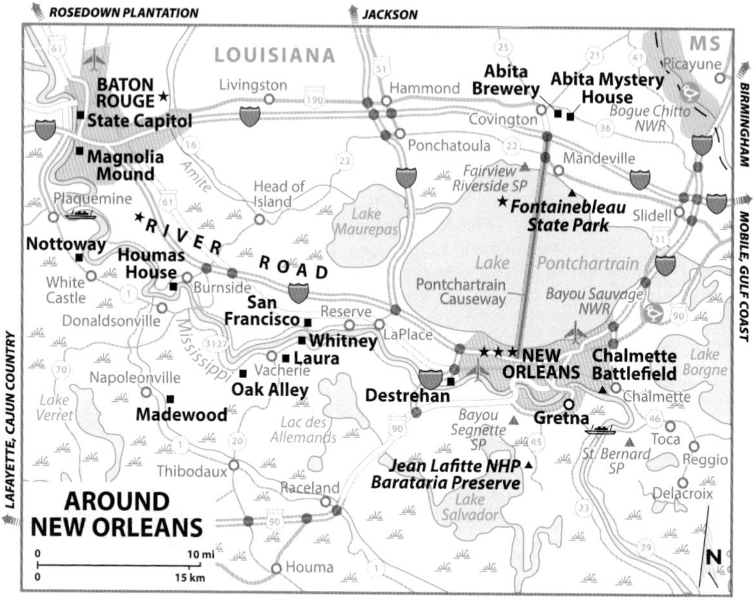

AROUND NEW ORLEANS

DESTREHAN

13034 River Rd., Destrehan. 985-764-9315. www.destrehanplantation.org.
Completed in 1790 as the heart of a 6,000-acre indigo (later sugarcane) plantation, this raised Creole-style manor is considered the oldest documented plantation house in the Mississippi Valley.
In 1793, it was purchased by Jean Noel Destrehan who, with his brother-in-law Etienne de Boré, perfected the process of granulating sugar. The house was expanded in 1810, and Greek Revival ornamental details were added in 1839 to conform to antebellum tastes. Historic craft demonstrations (indigo-dyeing, candlemaking) take place daily.

SAN FRANCISCO

2646 Hwy. 44, Garyville. 985-535-2341. www.sanfranciscoplantation.org.
The eye-catching exterior style of this ebulliently decorated plantation house (1856), with its latticework, scrolled cornices and balustraded captain's walk, was dubbed "Steamboat Gothic" style for its fancied resemblance to riverboats passing on the Mississippi. The interior is restored to c.1860.

HOUMAS HOUSE

40136 Hwy. 942, Burnside. ℘225-473-9380. www.houmashouse.com.
This stately plantation home gained its name from the land it was built upon, which was originally owned by the Houmas Indians.
Houmas pairs a modest four-room c.1790 house with an 1840 Greek Revival mansion built for John Smith Preston, a son-in-law of Revolutionary War hero Wade Hampton. The stunning gardens nurture native Louisiana and exotic tropical plants.

NOTTOWAY

31025 Hwy. 1, White Castle. ℘225-545-2730. www.nottoway.com.
Largest plantation home in the South, this ornate white mansion (1859) on the Mississippi displays a fanciful mix of Greek Revival and Italianate styles. Designed by Henry Howard for Virginia sugarcane planter John Hampden Randolph and his family, the 53,000sq ft house boasts 64 rooms sporting elegant appointments. .

OAK ALLEY

3645 Hwy. 18, Vacherie. ℘225-265-2151. www.oakalleyplantation.com.
Named for the gracious quarter-mile-long alléea of 28 live oak trees that approaches it on the river side, this stately Greek Revival mansion was completed in 1839 as the heart of a flourishing sugarcane plantation. (The trees predate the house by more than a century.) A total of 28 massive

San Francisco

columns support the two-story gallery surrounding the house. The interior is furnished with fine period antiques.

LAURA

2247 Hwy. 18, Vacherie. ℘225-265-7690. www.lauraplantation.com. -
The Creole culture of New Orleans and the lower Mississippi Valley are the focus of excellent guided tours of this colorfully painted raised Creole cottage (1805). Also on the site are 12 historic outbuildings, including original slave cabins where, in the 1870s, the African folktales of Br'er Rabbit were first recorded.

BATON ROUGE★

H1-2 *80 miles from New Orleans on 1-10W.*
Incorporated in 1817, this busy port and and university city on the banks of the Mississippi has been Louisiana's state capital since 1849. Its colorful name comes from the "red stick" placed by local Indians to mark a hunting boundary.

Louisiana's State Capitol building (*State Capitol Dr. at N. 4th St.; ℘225-219-1200; www.crt.state.la.us*), a striking 34-story Art Deco skyscraper (1932), is the tallest state capitol in the US. It dominates the surrounding landscape, as was the intention of its creator, the controversial and redoubtable governor Huey P. Long. Long was buried in the Capitol's garden after being assassinated in 1935. Views from the spire's 27th-floor observation deck encompass the river and the Pentagon barracks, established in 1819 to house a US army garrison serving the southwestern US. **The Old Arsenal** (1838) situated amid pretty gardens to the east of the spire, contains a small military museum.

Capitol Park Museum

660 N. 4th St. - *℘225-342-5428 - www.louisianastatemuseum.org.*
The sleek modern building across from the capitol contains colorful, fun exhibits about the state's history, economy and culture. Look for the Civil War-era submarine, or try your feet at dancing to zydeco or Cajun music.

Old State Capitol

100 North Blvd. - ℘225-342-0500 - www.louisianaoldstatecapitol.org.
At this castle-like, Gothic Revival-style structure (1850), representatives in 1861 voted to withdraw from the Union and form a separate nation (it existed for four weeks). Today the building has displays on Louisiana's colorful political history.
A concrete promenade along the east bank of the river near the Old State Capitol makes for a pleasant stroll past riverboat casinos and the USS Kidd /, a decommissioned World War II destroyer *(305 S. River Rd.; ℘225-342-1942).*

Louisiana Art & Science Museum

100 River Rd - ℘225-344-5272 - www.lasm.org. This riverfront structure mounts good temporary exhibits on artistic and cultural themes. A permanent Egypt gallery intrigues with its full-size mummy. In the planetarium you can explore space exhibits and take in a show in the domed theater.

Magnolia Mound Plantation

2161 Nicholson Dr. - ℘225-343-4955 - www.friendsofmagnoliamound.org.
Visitors may view an open-hearth cooking demonstration in the working detached kitchen before touring the gracious house (c.1791), considered one of the finest examples of Creole-style architecture in the area.

Rosedown Plantation State Historic Site

12501 Hwy. 10, 26mi north of Baton Rouge off US-61, St. Francisville -

© Louisiana Office of Tourism/Tim Mueller Photography

Formal garden, Rosedown Plantation State Historic Site

℘225-635-3332 - www.crt.state.la.us. Don't miss this faithfully restored Greek Revival-style home (1835) and its 28-acre historic formal gardena where owner Daniel Turnbull's wife, Martha, experimented with exotic plant species, successfully introducing azaleas and camellias to the southeastern US.

WHERE TO EAT AND STAY IN RIVER ROAD

Roberto's River Road Restaurant– *1985 LA-75, Sunshine, LA - ℘225 642 5999 - www.robertosrestaurant.net - Tue- Fri 11am-2pm; Tue-Thu. 5pm-9pm; Fri.-Sat. 5pm-10pm.* Dishes at this homey seafood shack have some refined touches: take the eggplant crabcakes in Roberto's buerre blanc, or the fresh gulf fish served in papillote, with lemon a fresh herbs. Don't miss Roberto's shrimp dishes, like the river road shrimp: the most succulent gulf shrimp sauteed in spicy brandy butter and garlic, served in a bread bowl of french baguette.

Madewood Plantation House – *4250 Hwy. 308, Napoleonville - ℘985 369 7151 or ℘800-375-7151 - www.madewood.com - 8 rooms.* This 1846 Greek Revival mansion sits in the middle of an active sugarcane plantation 75mi from New Orleans. Period antiques, including scrolled canopy, fourposter and half-tester beds, add authenticity. Breakfast, evening wine and cheese in the library, and candlelit dinners around the dining room's huge oak table are part of the deal. Private dining in the Music Room can be reserved in advance.

St. Ann

Addresses

Cafe du Monde
© Jason Langley/age fotostock

Where to eat

Find the addresses on our maps using the numbers in the listing (ex. 1). The coordinates in red (ex. C2) refer to the detachable map (inside the cover).

FRENCH QUARTER

Area map p. 19

Picnic idea – *Find a bench along the Mississippi River and watch the barges pass by.*

Under $15

1 **Acme Oyster House** – ***F6*** – *724 Iberville St., - ✆504 522 5973 - www.acmeoyster.com - daily 10:30am-10pm - lunch $9-15 - dinner $10-16.* Though often crowded, this is still one of the best places for the quintessential Crescent City lunch, an oyster (or shrimp) po-boy sandwich.

1 **Central Grocery** – ***F6*** – *923 Decatur St., - ✆504 523 1620 - www.centralgrocery.com - daily 9am-5pm - $11-15.* A French Quarter staple, the storefront serves oversized sandwiches served in gritty, historic digs. Central Grocery's claim to fame is the muffuletta sandwich, invented in the shop: a large, round sandwich of homemade bread, cured meats, and Italian olive salad. Open since 1906, the third generation of the Sicilian immigrant family still own and operate the store.

1 **Coop's Place** – ***F6*** – *1109 Decatur St., ✆504 525 9053 - www.coopsplace.net - 11am-12am (1am Fri and Sat) - $10-15.* Join the long line outside this Decatur Street eatery if you're craving Cajun comfort food at very comfortable prices. This ultra-popular, no frills restaurant serves any type of seafood imaginable, fried, jambalaya, Cajun-inspired pastas, and dishes of Redfish.

1 **Killer PoBoys** – ***F6*** – *219 Dauphine St., - ✆504 462 2731 - www.killerpoboys.com -10am-8pm - Closed Tue - $11-15.* This sandwich shop takes traditions to a new level, with international and modern ingredients like glazed pork belly, smoked salmon, and roasted cauliflower reinventing the New Orleans' classic po' boy sandwich. Wash it down with a cold, local beer.

Changing prices

Formal restaurants often feature weekday lunches with prix fixe menus for around $20-30, with drink specials and multiple courses. It's easy to find po boys and other casual lunch options for under $15. Dinner options range from $20 entrees to $50 for prime steak cuts, whole fish, or other specialty seafood options. Price categories reflect that of a typical entree and do not include tip (typical gratiuty in the US includes %15-20 of the bill for table service).

Port of Call – ***F6*** - *838 Esplanade Ave. - ✆504 523 0121 - www.portofcallnola.com - daily 11am-12pm - 11am-1am weekends - $10-14.* Locals and tourists go crazy for the over-the-top burgers at this crowded, rowdy pub on Esplanade avenue. Come hungry (the burgers are huge) and be prepared to wait in line outside with the (often drunken) masses.

$20-$30

Angeline – ***F6*** – *1032 Chartres St. - ✆504 308 3106- www.angelinenola.com - closed Mon, Tue - dinner 5:30pm -10:30pm; Fri-Sun 10am-2pm, 5:30-10:30pm - $17-25.* A relative newcomer to the contemporary American dining scene in the French Quarter, Chef Alex Harrell (previously of Bayona, Ralphs on the Park, and Sylvain) opened Angeline in 2015. Here the team pairs wine and cocktails with a menu of Mediterranean and southern inspired dishes, served in The simple yet elegant dining room. Brunch is also a great time to indulge here.

Bayona – ***F6*** – *430 Dauphine St., ✆504 525 4455 - www.bayona.com - lunch 11:30am-1pm - dinner 5:30pm -9:30pm - $11-15.* Nationally-renowned chef-owner Susan Spicer creates an exciting menu of international flavors rooted in Southern traditions. The former cottage maintains its charm, with a brick-walled and plant-covered courtyard for outdoor seating.

Café Amelie – ***F6*** - *912 Royal St., ✆504 412 8965 - www.cafeamelie.com - 11am-9pm - Closed Mon and Tue - $15-26.* Flowers, a trickling fountain and tropical plants grace the courtyard entrance at this cafe, welcoming guests into a charmed, romantic dining experience. The small dining room opens its doors onto the cobblestone courtyard most nights, so either way you are dining al fresco. The menu includes elevated Creole favorites and decadent eggs benedict renditions at brunch, accompanied by fresh cocktails and an extensive wine list.

Court of Two Sisters – ***F6*** – *613 Royal St., - ✆504 522 7261 - www.courtoftwosisters.com- 9am-3pm; 5pm-10pm.* The best way to enjoy this iconic, old school spot is during a daily jazz brunch. The brunch buffet serves decadent New Orleans favorites seafood creole omelettes made to order, ettouffee, sweet potato andouille sausage, bananas foster, and bread pudding. A fun crowd of tourists, and some celebrating locals, bask in the life light and music of one of the favorite courtyards in the city. At $30 for each adult, it's a good way to get a lot of flavors of the French Quarter (indulgent food, jazz music, and gorgeous old courtyard) in one go.

Galatoire's – ***F6*** – *209 Bourbon Street - ✆504 525 4455 - www.galatoires.com - lunch 11:30am-10pm - Closed Mon - $25-35.* Jean Galatoire first opened the restaurant's doors in 1905, serving rustic dishes from his hometown village of Pardies, France. Five generations later, the service is a bit more dusty than it used to be, but it's worth a trip to this historic dining room for the Oysters Rockefeller and Crabmeat Yvonne (jumbo lump crabmeat in a sauce of artichokes and mushrooms).

1 **Meauxbar** – ***F6*** – *942 N Rampart St., ☏504 569 9979 - www.meauxbar.com - dinner 5pm-10pm - brunch weekends 10:30am-2pm - $20-30.* Local ingredients shine at this small corner bistro, with dark wood floors and leather booths. Expect fresh, exciting renditions of culinary classics like escargot and steak au poivre.

1 **Sylvain** – ***F6*** – *625 Chartres St., ☏504 265 8123 - www.sylvainnola.com - dinner 5:30pm-11pm - brunch weekends 10:30am - $15-25.* The team behind a few chic spots around town (Meauxbar, Cavan, and Barrelproof) transformed a 1770s carriage house into an intimate gastropub. The menu is equal parts comfort and elegance, with a hearty pub burger and handcut fries served alongside entrees like veal sweetbreads, beef cheeks, and papardelle bolognese.

1 **Trinity Restuarant** – ***F6*** – *1117 Decatur St., ☏504 325 5789 - trinityrestaurantneworleans.com - Tue-Thu 4:30-10pm; Fri 3pm-11pm; Sat and Sun 11am-10pm; closed Mon.- $15-25.* The best way to experience Chef Mike Isolani's modern Creole cuisine is surrounded by drag queens on a Saturday morning. This new restaurant in town has already become popular for its drag brunch, with quality egg dishes and specialty Creole plates, and $14 bottomless mimosas.

Over $30

6 **Arnaud's** – ***E5*** – *813 Bienville St., - ☏504 523 5433- www.arnaudsrestaurant.com - 6-10pm daily - dinner $30-35.* One of New Orleans' cherished old-line culinary favorites, Arnaud's serves dishes that embody the pinnacle of fine Creole cuisine. Try mouthwatering duck breast with blueberry sauce, Oysters Bienville (simmered with shrimp, green onions and mushrooms) or tender pompano, perfectly seasoned. Try a café brulot (flavored with spices and flamed) with your desserts.

6 **Mr. B's Bistro** – ***E5*** – *201 Royal St. ☏504 523 2078- www.mrbsbistro.com - 11:30am-9pm daily - lunch $18-25 - dinner $35.* A French Quarter supper club known for its contemporary spin on local favorites. Mr.B's BBQ shrimp in a fiery pepper sauce and Gumbo Ya Ya (a soupy version of hearty chicken-and-andouille sausage stew) keep fans coming back. Bread pudding is the signature dessert.

1 **Restaurant R'Evolution** – ***F6*** – *Royal Sonesta Hotel, 777 Bienville St., - ☏504 553 2277 - www.revolutionnola.com - dinner 5:30pm-10pm; Friday lunch 11:30am-2:30pm; Sunday brunch 10:30am-2pm - $35-60.* The elegant dining experience at Restaurant R'Evolution juxtaposes its proximity to an often crowded and wild section of Bourbon Street. The service is formal and top notch, with wide, adjoining dining rooms each a little different than the next (the private room by the kitchen is the ultimate luxe experience). With a loaded menu of caviar, select steak cuts, and its own cellar of premier wines, this is the spot to splurge on your trip.

CENTRAL BUSINESS DISTRICT AND WAREHOUSE DISTRICT

Under $15

1 **Carmo** - ***F6*** - *527 Julia St., - 504 875 4132 -www.cafecarmo.com - 9am-10pm - Closed Sun - Lunch only Mon - $7-15.* A vegetarian-friendly, unique choice for fresh juices and inventive dishes at a reasonable price. The friendly cafe serves tropical and Latin American-inspired dishes, and the attached gallery space for browsing make it a great stop while touring the Warehouse District.

1 **Mother's** - ***F6*** - *401 Poydras St. - 504 523 9656 - www.mothers restaurant.net - 7am-10pm - $13.* This hole-in-the-wall is a favorite for fried seafood po' boys, greasy breakfast platters. Known for their baked ham, the kitchen also serves up hearty bowls of the classics like etouffee, red beans and rice, and jambalaya.

$20-30

1 **Cochon** - ***F6*** - *930 Tchoupitoulas St., - 504 588 2123 - www.cochon restaurant.com - 11am-10pm - $24.* While the menu at this lively, popular dinner destination centers around Cajun renditions of pork, other proteins like the rabbit and dumplings, and fried alligator appetizer, shine as well. Next door, Cochon Butcher offers sandwiches, lunch fare and cocktails of the same high quality.

1 **Compère Lapin** - ***F6*** - *535 Tchoupitoulas St., - 504 599 2119 - www.comperelapin.com - Daily 5:30pm-10pm - Mon-Fri Lunch 11:30am-2:30pm - Sat and Sun Brunch 10:30am-2pm - $30.* French for "brother rabbit," of Caribbean folktales, Compere Lapin is a fine-dining restaurant in the lofty, industrial lobby of the Old No. 77 Hotel. The menu combines flavors of chef Nina Compton's childhood in St. Lucia with gourmet French and Italian influence, resulting in bold, flavorful dishes. Try the curried goat with sweet potato gnocchi, shrimp in Calabrian chili butter, or conch croquettes with pickled pineapple.

1 **Domenica** - ***F6*** - *123 Baronne St., - 504 648 6020 - www.domenica restaurant.com - 11am-11pm - $19-32.* Locals flock to Domenica for its happy hour, with daily drink specials and half-off pizzas. Other favorites include the burrata, housemade charcuterie, and fresh pastas, served in a contemporary and airy atmosphere.

1 **La Boca** - ***F6*** - *870 Tchoupitoulas St., - 504 525 8205 - www.laboca steaks.com - Mon-Wed 5:30pm-10pm - Weekends 5:30pm-12am - $31-60.* This Argentine-style steakhouse serves prime filets and skirt steak alongside bottles of malbec and proveleta, a traditional melted cheese appetizer. The ambiance here is warm and inviting.

89 **Maypop** - ***E4*** - *611 O'Keefe Ave. - 504 518 6345 - www.maypop restaurant.com - 11am-10pm - $18-27.* Started by favorite local young chef Mike Gulotta, Maypop isn't like any other food you'll taste in New Orleans. Small plates feature Southeast Asian flavors, fresh roti, marinated shrimp, and homemade pastas and noodles. Weekend brunch includes a dim sum-style menu.

(1) **Pêche** - ***F6*** - *800 Magazine St., - 504 522 1744 - www.pecherestaurant.com - 11am-10pm - $26.* Local seafood is the word at restaurateur Donald Link's renowned restaurant. The atmosphere is corporate and bustling, but the menu makes it worth the wait in line for a table. The raw bar and small plates selections, like the spicy shrimp and hand-pulled noodles, select gulf oysters, or the towering seafood platter, are where gulf delicacies really shine.

(1) **Seaworthy** - ***F6*** - *630 Carondelet St, 504 930 3071 - www.seaworthynola.com - Mon–Fri: 4pm–2am; Sat–Sun: 11am–2am - $15-25.* An oyster bar and seafood restuarant, with a great oyster happy hour that features cream-of-the-crop gulf oysters, from Murder Point, Grand Isle and Area 3, far from what you'll get in some of the more touristy joints near Bourbon Street. The atmosphere is chic and refined. Every Tuesday night, for less than $30, the restuarant throws a family style, prix fixe "crew mess" dinner.

LOWER GARDEN DISTRICT AND CENTRAL CITY

Area map p. 31

Under $15

(9) **Casa Borrega** - ***F5*** - *1719 Oretha Castle Haley Blvd. - 504 427 0654 - -www.casaborrega.com -11am-9:30pm (10:30pm weekends); closed Mon - $14-22.* A longtime favorite of the OC Haley arts and culture area of Central City, the owners, chefs. and bartenders, hailing from Mexico City and elsewhere in Central America, serve delicious tacos, margaritas, and a variety of mezcals. There's live latin music almost nightly and a colorful courtyard for al fresco dining.

(13) **Turkey and the Wolf** - ***F4*** - *739 Jackson Ave. - 09 52 55 11 66 - www.turkeyandthewolf.com - 11am-5pm - Closed Tue - $10.50.* While surprising that a kitschy sandwich shop started by fun-loving transplants would win *Bon Apetit Magazine's* 2017 Best Restaurant of the Year (and much national press following), the inventive comfort food here doesn't disappoint. Chefs take classic American luncheon food (bologna sandwich, wedge salad, deviled eggs) and up the game with fresh ingredients and house-cured meats.

$20-30

(12) **Emeril's Delmonico Restaurant and Bar** - ***G4*** - *1300 St. Charles Ave. - 504 525 4937 - www.emerilsrestaurants.com - Daily 5pm-9pm (10pm Fri and Sat) - $28-33.* When celebrity chef Emeril Lagasse restored the former Delmonico restaurant, he framed the 18ft windows in ultra suede and velvet panels, covered the walls with neutral shades of grass cloth, linen and cotton and updated the menus with modern twists on traditional Creole cuisine. Located on the edge of the Garden District, Delmonico features such updated classics as crabcakes with mango butter and cucumber kimchi; Louisiana drumfish Meuniere and jerk-spiced lamb sirloin with rum-glazed yams.

Toups South – ***F5*** - *1504 Oretha Castle Haley Blvd. - ☏504 304 2147 - www.toupssouth.com -11am-10pm (11pm weekends) Closed Tue - 10am-3pm Sun - $16-28.* As a contestant on Bravo's *Top Chef* Season 13, James Beard-winning Chef Isaac Toups quickly became a crowd favorite for his down-to-earth Cajun spirit and cooking style . The atmosphere at Toups South (adjoining the Southern Food and Beverage Museum) is slightly more refined than Toups Meatery, his first restaurant in Mid City, but the food, based in his rustic Cajun roots, still shines, from the boudin (fresh sausage with rice and spices) to gulf stew and crab salad.

GARDEN DISTRICT

Under $15

(89) **Cowbell** - ***E4*** - *8801 Oak St., - ☏504 866 4222 - www.cowbell-nola.com - Tue–Thur 11:30 am–9:00 pm; Fri and Sat 11:30 am–10:00 pm - Closed Sun and Mon. - $11-18.* Tulane students and Uptown locals can attest to how good the burgers are at this homey joint in a former gas station towards the riverbend. Kitschy, recycled decor, homemade pie and ice cream, and more-than-reasonable prices all make it worth a visit.

(70) **Dat Dog** - ***F7*** - *3336 Magazine St. - ☏504 324 2226 - www.datdog.com - daily 11am-10pm. (11pm Fri and Sat) (9pm Sun) - $8* This souped-up, brightly colored hot dog stand specializes in unique dogs, like turducken, andouille or alligator sausages piled with unlimited toppings of your choice. They also serve local beer and loaded fries. Pick from a menu of curated dogs or let one of the hawaiian shirt-clad staff members dress your meal to their choosing.

(21) **Domilise's Po-Boy & Bar** – ***F7*** - *5240 AnnunciationSt. - ☏504 899 9126 - www.domilisespoboys.com - - 10am-6:30pm, Sat 10:30am-7pm - $9-13.* Line up along the sidewalk for these colossal po boys of roast beef, turkey and fried seafood, overflowing on fresh french bread and wrapped in butcher paper. You might be luck to get a seat at a mismatched table in the dining room, decorated with beer signs, newspaper articles, and old photos of the historic sandwich shop; but you'll be just as happy enjoying your meal on a stoop or street corner like many other diners.

(71) **Stien's Deli** - ***E6*** - *2207 Magazine St. - ☏504 527 0771 - www.steins deli.com - Tue-Fri 7am-7pm - Sat and Sun 9am-5pm - Closed Mon - $8-12.* The Philadelphia-style delicatessen serves the best of deli food, like reubens, smoked fish spreads, and matzoh ball soup, alongside a menu of creative sandwiches. The digs are authentically no-frills and grungy (as is the gruff counter service). Cherry Espresso operates a coffee counter in the front, and there's a large selection of rare ales and microbrews in the back.

$20-30

(89) **Casamento's** - ***E4*** - *4330 Magazine St. - ☏504 895 9761 - www.casamentosrestaurant.com - Closed Mon-Wed; Thur-Sun 11am-2pm,*

5:30pm-9pm. Diners looking for an old school, seafood joint vibe new orleans is known for, complete with tiled floors, bistro tables, and waiters who have been around for 30 years, will be happy to venture out of the French Quarter and find Casamento's. Oyster shuckers are hard at work at this narrow, mosaic-tiled restaurant, and it's best to order your first dozen while waiting for a table. Entrees include heaping piles of delicately fried seafood.

17 **Commander's Palace** – ***E6*** – *1403 Washington Ave. - ✆504 899 8221 - www.commanderspalace.com - Lunch 11:30pm-1:30pm, Dinner 6pm-1:30am - Lunch only Sat and Sun*. Still enforcing a dress code for gentleman (no shorts, even in summer), this venerable bastion of elegance in the Garden District not only serves excellent modern Creole cuisine (veal sweetbreads with pear and Chablis jam), it also provides unsurpassed service. It's often listed among the best restaurants in the country.

19 **Coquette** – ***F6*** – *2800 Magazine St. - ✆504 265 0421 - www.coquettenola.com - daily 5:30pm-10pm; weekend brunch 10:30-2pm - $20-32*. This gorgeous corner restaurant wows diners with a menu of fresh ingredients prepared with intuitive technique (vegetable crudite with smoked catfish dip, turnip bottarga, fennel soubise). Dive into a five-course blind tasting menu for the ultimate experience. The narrow, chandeliered dining room is refined but petite, and reservations are recommended.

23 **Le Petite Grocery** – ***H8*** – *4238 Magazine St. - ✆504 891 3377 - www.lapetitegrocery.com - Lunch 11:30am-2pm, Dinner 5:30pm-10:30pm - No lunch Mon - $25-30*. An elegant corner restuarant by James Beard-award winning chef Justin Devillier. Consistent crowd favorites are the turtle bolognese and blue crab beignets .

23 **Shaya** – ***H8*** – *4213 Magazine St - ✆504 891 4213 - www.shaya restaurant.com - Daily 11am-10pm - $20-25*. Israeli cuisine might not scream New Orleans to you, but this award-winning restaurant is one of the best meals you'll find on Magazine Street and beyond. The chic, airy eatery, with its white tiles and minimalist decor, is best known for inventive hummus and share plates. Served alongside is their addictive pita bread, cooked in an authentic wood-burning oven in the corner of the dining room.

UPTOWN AND CARROLTON AVE.

Area map p.34

89 **Avo** – ***E4*** – *5908 Magazine St. - ✆504 509 6550 - www.restaurant avo.com - Mon-Sat 5pm-10pm; Brunch Sat-Sun 10:30am-2pm - $18*. Guests in this romantic dining room look out onto the brickwalled candlelit courtyard as they enjoy fresh italian dishes like charred octopus, salumi, and cacio e pepe. Chef Nick Lima, raised in New Orleans and third generation Sicilian, pays tribute to his grandparents in a delicious and

sophisticated way that has garnered national attention.

25 **Boucherie** - ***DE5*** - *1506 S. Carrollton Ave. - ✆504 862 5514 - www.boucherie-nola.com - Lunch Tue–Sat 11am-3pm, Dinner Mon–Sat 5:30pm-9:30pm, Brunch Sun 10:30am-2:30pm.* It's worth a trek Uptown to experience the best of contemporary Southern food, served in this cozy dining room of a converted shotgun house. Chef Nathaniel Zamet's creative menu, with Asian, Creole, and French influences, changes frequently, but few staples, like the boudin balls, wagyu brisket and the krispy kreme bread pudding for dessert, are can't-miss. Keep an eye out for their exciting tasting menus and specialty dinners. Next door, Bouree, their casual sister, serves wings, snacks and craft cocktail-style daiquiris.

29 **La Crepe Nanou** - ***D6*** - *1410 Robert St. - ✆504 899 2670 - www.lacrepenanou.com - Daily 5pm-10pm - Brunch Sun 11am-3pm.* Behind the velvet maroon curtains of this uptown bistro's doorway is a casual, French-flair dining room with original paintings of Garden District scenes. On the menu: typical bistro fare with a New Orleans twist, as well as authentic classic moules frites.

74 **Dante's Kitchen** - ***DE6*** - *736 Dante St. - ✆504 861 3121 - www.danteskitchen.com - Closed Tue - Dinner 6pm-9:15pm; brunch weekends 10:30am-2pm - $20-25.* A reminder that good food in New Orleans doesn't have to come with a bow-tied waiter and prix fixe menu, Dante's Kitchen serves consistently delicious Southern dishes in a colorful, down-to-earth setting. Shrimp and grits, biscuits, and bloody marys draw crowds to the weekend brunch, but the pork belly with kimchi, escargot and bone marrow, and chicken-under-a-brick are appeals of the dinner menu as well.

32 **Dick & Jenny's** - ***D6*** - *4501 Tchoupitoulas St. - ✆504 894 9880 - www.dickandjennys.com - 5pm-9pm - Closed Mon and Tue* - $19-25. You feel you've stepped in for a home-cooked meal at your best friend's house in this Uptown cottage. Best bets on the eclectic menu: the shrimp and grits, Louisiana flounder with sweet potato grits, or any of the gumbos du jour.

30 **Jaques-Imo's** - ***E6*** - *8324 Oak St., - ✆504 861 0886 - 5pm-10pm (10:30pm Fri and Sat) - Closed Sun - $30.* With wild paint covering every surface, an effusive owner and a dedicated crowd of regulars, this Uptown spot wins points for its funky ambiance and delicious local fare, such as expertly cooked fish or steak dishes.

28 **Patois** - ***D6*** - *26078 Laurel St. - ✆504 895 9441 - www.patoisnola.com - 5:30-10pm (10:30pm Fri and Sat, Brunch Sun 10:30pm-2pm, Lunch Fri 11:30am-2pm - $19-26.* On a corner of a quiet residential Uptown street, this charming bistro features rustic French and Creole dishes for dinner daily, Friday lunch and Sunday brunch. The warm but chic setting provides a romantic escape from downtown bustle.

75 Upperline - ***D7*** - *1413 Upperline St.- ✆504 891 9822 - www.upperline.com - Wed-Sun 5:30pm-9pm - prix fixe dinners $40/$48.* Owner JoAnn Clevenger makes you feel like a guest at a neighborhood dinner party at this cottage filled with quirky local art. The host presides over the white-tablecloth tables, chatting with guests and giving recommendations from the menu of vibrant New Orleans fare.

THE FAUBOURG MARIGNY AND BYWATER

Under $15

36 Bywater Bakery - ***B5*** - 3624 Dauphine St. - *✆504 336 3336 - www.bywaterbakery.com - daily 7am-5pm - $8* This homey neighborhood cafe, with walls full of local art, and afternoon live music, serves coffee, homemade pastries, pies and king cakes to take home. A heartier lunch menu offers soups, salads and open-faced sandwich on homemade bread (the mushroom toast is divine).

78 Elizabeth's - ***D6*** - 601 Gallier St. - *✆504 944 9272 - www.elizabethsrestaurantnola.com - daily 8am-2:30pm, 5pm-10pm - $13.* Known best for their brunch, with Praline bacon, indulgent *pain perdu* and bloody marys, the experience at Elizabeth's is friendly and colorful, with an authentic neighborhood vibe. Walk to Crescent Park across the street after brunch for views of the Mississippi River.

77 The Joint - ***C6*** - *701 Mazant St. - ✆504 949 3232 - www.alwayssmokin.com - 11:30am-10pm - Closed Sun - $14.* You'll smell the smoker long before you reach the screened doors of this barbeque shack, where piles of expertly smoked brisket, chicken and ribs, and mouth-watering sides do not disappoint.

1 Pizza Delicious - ***F6*** - *617 Piety St., ✆504 676 8482- pizzadelicious.com - 11am-11pm; closed Mon - $15-20.* This Bywater staple sells the best thin crust, New York-style pizza in New Orleans. Over the last few years, the young chefs here have honed their skill to turn out some delicious fresh pastas and salads as well. Casual counter service and a hip local crowd make it a fun spot to grab dinner.

1 Red's Chinese - ***F6*** - *3048 St Claude Ave. - ✆504 304 6030 - www.redschinese.com - 12pm-11pm - $15-20.* inspired by San Francisco's Mission Chinese Restuarant, this delightfully "Hipster Chinese" place serves craft cocktails, and messy, spice-forward plates of Chinese classics-with-a-spin.

1 Sneaky Pickle - ***F6*** - *4017 St Claude Ave, ✆504 218 5651 - www.yousneakypickle.com - 9am-9:30pm - $15-25.* Meat lover's shouldn't write off the mostly-vegan menu here, where dishes are anything but bland. Take the rueben, or the mac n' cheese: both vegan, but chock-full of umami, and creamy, savory goodness. The restaurant often features "real meat" flatbreads and other carnivorous specials. Beer and wine options are affordable, and the courtyard is pleasant.

Elizabeth's

ELIZABETH'S
REAL FOOD DONE REAL GOOD
601 Gallier 944-9272
AFOOD
AILY
GOING BUT HURRY BACK
TAKE YOUR TIME GOING BUT HURRY BACK
PO BOYS
REDNECK
EGGS
CREOLE
EAT
Eat
GUARD DOG
ON DUTY
Yes we are
OPEN!

1 St. Roch Market – ***F6*** – *2381 St Claude Ave, ☎504 609 38133 - www.strochmarket.com - dinner 7am-10pm (11pm) - $15-18.* The story of St. Roch Market has a lot to say about population trends in the neighborhood. This building began as a community grocery, before laying in blight for years. After extensive renovations it reopened in is now a hip, gourmet food hall showcases local vendors and their talents. Enjoy new-wave New Orleans delicacies from vegan bowls to empanadas to rotisserie chicken sandwiches. There is an oyster bar and fresh seafood stand, as well as a full liquor bar.

Around $20

37 Adolfo's – ***C6*** – 611 Frenchmen St. - *6pm-10pm - Closed Sun - $11-30.* A small dining room perched above the Apple Barrel music club, Adolfo's serves Creole-Italian food to cramped tables over red-and-white checkered tablecloths and candlelight. They're specialty is fresh seafood or meat, drenched in one of their classic sauces. Cash only. You will leave happy and reeking of garlic.

35 Paladar 511 – ***B5*** – *511 Marigny St. - ☎504 509 6782 - www.paladar511.com - dinner 5:30pm-10:30pm, brunch 10am-2pm weekends.* Hi-top tables, intimate booths and a large bar fill this industrial space, with high ceilings and ton of natural light. While the menu is based on homey Italian choices like ravioli, pizza, and arancini, complex, bright dishes are anything but ordinary.

37 N7 – ***C6*** – 1117 Montegut St. - *6pm-10pm - Closed Sun - $11-30.* Tucked away on a small Bywater side street, this pint-sized European bistro is worth finding. The kitchen specializes in rare, imported canned seafood and other goods, mostly from Spain, served alongside a warm baguette, a negroni or light glass of Bordeaux.

MID CITY AND BAYOU ST. JOHN

Under $15

1 1000 Figs – ***F6*** – *3141 Ponce De Leon St #1, ☎504 301 0848 - www.1000figs.com - 11am-9pm; Closed Sun and Mon - $14.* delicious falafel, mezze, lamb and chicken sandwiches, and fried brussel sprouts. Pile in to this small, hip dining room covered in unfinished wood, wait for a much coveted sidewalk table, or take your fare next door, to the Swirl Wine Bar, where you can truly have it all.

80 Blue Oak BBQ – ***B2*** – *900 N. Carrollton Ave. - ☎504 822 2583 - www.blueoakbbq.com - 11am-9pm - Closed Mon - $16.* New Orleans natives Phil Moseley and Ronnie Evans travelled far and wide to learn the best techniques of American BBQ, then returned home to open an authentic joint with the best brisket, ribs, and smoked meats you'll find in the deep south. The bar serves draft beers from local breweries.

44 Marjie's Grill – ***B3*** – *320 S. Broad Ave. - ☎ 504 603 2234 - www.marjiesgrill.com - Lunch 11am-2:30pm - Dinner 5:30pm-10pm - No lunch Sat - Closed Sun - $14-22.* Foodies flock to this casual eatery on an unassuming block of South Broad St., where chefs showcase a unique use of Gulf South and Southeast Asian flavors. Dishes like local catch marinated in Asian chili and satsuma, charred pork shoulder with tumeric, and wintermelon salad all make up the eclectic menu. Staff favorite wines and craft cocktails are served in assorted thrift store glasses.

1 **Mid City Pizza** - ***F6*** - *4400 Banks St. 504 483 8609 - www.midcitypizza.com - 11am-12am- $16.* This friendly neighborhood joint takes cues from the 90s in decor (think Ninja Turtles and NBA Jams), but not in taste. Beer choices are local and fresh, the regular pie is ultra-satisfying. and inventive specials are fun to try.

42 **Parkway Bakery & Tavern** - ***C4*** - *538 Hagan Ave. - 504 482 3047* - www.*parkwaypoorboys.com - 11am-10pm; closed Tue - $14.* Some of the best po' boys in town with a fun bar and outdoor seating area. For the full experience-in-one, order a surf and turf: combines the roast beef debris (dripping fresh beef in gravy) and fried gulf shrimp in one giant sandwich. Look for specials, like Monday night fried oyster po boys, or Wednesdays in fall, when locals join a long line for the thanksgiving leftovers po' boy.

Around $20

43 **Cafe Degas** - ***E4*** - *3127 Esplanade Ave. - 504 945 5635 - www.cafedegas.com - Wed-Sun 11am-3pm, 5:30-10pmBrunch Sat 10:30am-3pm.* On the vine-covered deck overlooking Esplanade Ave., you'll feel (and eat) as if at a neighborhood Parisian cafe. Housemade charcuterie, escargot, and other classics are delicious and surprisingly affordable.

89 **Mandina's** - ***E4*** - *3800 Canal St. - 504 482 9179 - www.mandinasrestaurant.com. 11am-9:30pm (10pm Fri and Sat), 12pm-9pm Sun - $18.* A delightfully old school Mid City joint, Mandina's bowtied waiters serve up classic Creole soups (turtle, gumbo,oyster and artichoke) alongside fresh french bread, shrimp remoulade, and towering plates of weekday specials. Seriously hungry guest should indulge in the spaghetti and meatballs, or hamburger-served "on french" (po boy style).

OUT OF TOWN

New Orleans East

89 **Doung Phong** - ***E4*** - *14207 Chef Menteur Hwy - 504 254 0214 - dpbakeshop.com - 8am-5pm; Closed Tue - $7.* This unassuming Vietnamese bakery recently won a James Beard Classic Award for its consistent service and inspiration to the community. Come Mardi Gras, their king cakes are legendary and highly coveted. Chefs from all over New Orleans travel here to use their fresh baked french bread in their restaurants. The restaurant, serving traditional pho and vietnamese dishes, is good, but the real treat here is the bakery. Crowd in for a banh mi (around $3 for a french bread sandwich with pork, pate,

jalepenos, cilantro, and pickled carrots) and an assortment of sweet and savory pastries, steamed buns, and meat pies.

Northshore

89 **La Provence** - ***E4*** - *25020 US-190, Lacombe, LA - 985 626 7662 - www.laprovencerestaurant.com; Tue-Sat 5pm-9pm; Sun 11am-3pm; Closed Mon and Tues - $18.* Experience a rustic French kitchen with La Provence in Lacombe, LA, which, thirty minutes from New Orleans, feels decidedly much more country. The restaurant has its own working farm, complete with a garden and live stock, which you can tour while waiting for a table. The dining room is formal and romantic, with the french dishes you might expect: rabbit, roasts, ratatouille.

West Bank

89 **Salvo's** - ***E4*** - *7742 Hwy 23, Belle Chasse, LA - 504 393 7303 - www.salvosseafood.com - 8am-9pm; Closed Sun and Mon - $18.* Waiting in line for a table at Salvo's gives you a chance to really feel the neighborhood vibes of this place, about 45 minutes out of new orleans but arguably worth the trip. The real hit at Salvo's are the mouth-watering mounds of boiled seafood, featuring crawfish, shrimp, and crab legs. Wash it down with a cheap, light beer.

89 **Tan Dinh** - ***E4*** - *1705 Lafayette St. - 504 361 8008 - 10am-9pm; closed Tue - $14.* This large, casual Vietnamese spot is about 20 minutes from downtown New Orleans and serves some of the best pho (rice noodle soup with chicken or beef) in the area. The service is no-nonsense, and it's fun to watch nearby tables pile with Vietnamese specialties or unfamiliar dishes. For an appetizer, get the Tan Dinh special roll: a fried eggroll inside of a fresh spring roll.

89 **Tavolino** - ***E4*** - *141 Delaronde St., Algiers Point - 504 605 3365 - www.mandinasrestaurant.com. 3pm-9pm (10pm Thu-Sat); 11:30am-9pm Sun - $14.* While New Orleans hasn't traditionally been known for good pizza, Tavolino is perhaps an example that things are changing. Thin crust, 14-inch pies come with fresh goat cheese, drizzled in olive oil, chorizo, dates, or pleasantly simple margherita. The stuffed olives and arancini on the appetizer menu are highly recommended. Wine, beer, and specialty cocktails are served in the cozy bar.

89 **Tout de Suite** - ***E4*** - *347 Verret St. - 504 362 2264 - www.toutdesuitecafe.com - Tue-Sat 7am-4:30pm; Sun 7am–3pm; Mon 7am–12pm - $13.* An adorable neighborhood brunch spot serves towering plates of omelettes, eggs benedict, and different types of pancakes (try the sweet potato). The ultimate breakfast is the cajun special, with boudin and andouille gravy. They serve salads, sandwiches and soup for lunch.

Where to drink

New Orleans is truly a city of imbibing. Enjoy (in moderation): historic dive bars full of dilapidated charm, oak-paneled lounges serving decadent Ramos Gin Fizzes, and cafes with wide verandas for sipping chicory-laced cafe au laits under the live oaks.

Find the addresses on our maps using the number in the listing (ex. 1). The coordinates in red (ex. C2) refer to the detachable map (inside the cover).

THE FRENCH QUARTER

Area map p. 19

Cafés

2 **Cafe du Monde** - ***F6*** - *800 Decatur St. - 504 525 4544 - www.cafedumonde.com - Open 24 hrs.* For decades, the expert staff at this cafe have been dishing out hot plates of beignets (donut-like pastries covered in powdered sugar) and cafe au lait (chicory-flavored coffee with hot milk) to throngs of tourists under their green-and-white awnings by the French Market. A checkmark on any tourist's list, it's worth a trip for the beignets and coffee, which are still high quality, and excellent people watching. The cafe is open 24 hours, and just as good for an afternoon break as an end to a night out on Bourbon Street.

2 **Spitfire** - ***F6*** - *627 St Peter St. - 225 384 0655 - www.spitfirecoffee.com - Daily 8am-8pm.* This pint-size storefront serves local and boutique roasts, signature espresso drinks, pour-over coffee and small pastries.

Bars

6 **Black Penny**- ***E5*** - *700 N Rampart St. - 504 304 4779 - daily 12pm-4am.* A favorite among locals and service industry folks for their late nights and friendly bartenders, the high, cave-like walls of this tavern on rampart street display an impressive selection of canned and bottled beer from all over the world.

16 **Bar Tonique** – ***D4*** - *820 N Rampart St. - 504 324 6045 - www.bartonique.com - Daily 12pm-2am.* This cozy cocktail bar, with fireplaces and private booths, is often crowded with foot traffic from both locals and tourists from the French Quarter and nearby Armstrong Park. Fair-priced classic cocktails, daily drink specials, and expert, friendly bartenders are among its draws.

70 **Cane and Table** - ***D4*** - *1113 Decatur St. - 504 581 1112 - www.caneandtablenola.com - Daily 3pm-12am; Sat and Sun 10:30am-12am.* This elegant, Caribbean-themed bar is accompanied by a beautiful back courtyard, knowledgeable bartenders, and tiki drinks made from fresh juices and small batch spirits. The kitchen serves island-inspired small plates.

The Classics

New Orleans bartenders are among the best in the country. All pride themselves on their ability to churn out, with speed and skill, the famous cocktails that have been gracing New Orleans barrooms for decades (sometimes centuries). Order any of the following at a New Orleans bar and be prepared to be schooled on the exact methods of preparation for each traditional drink.

Sazerac *– Rye Whiskey, sugar, peychaud's bitters, lemon peeel, and a rinse of absinthe. Said to have been invented in New Orleans by Antoine Peychaude as one of the first cocktailsin the country.*

French 75 *– Gin or brandy, sugar, lemon, and sparkling wine. Came to New Orleans in the 1910s via Paris, and ahs been iconic to NOLA cocktail bars ever since*

Ramos Gin Fizz*-Egg whites, gin, sugar, cream, lemon, lime, orange flower water. A favorite drink of famous Louisiana governor Huey P. Long*

Vieux Carre*- brandy, rye, sweet vermouth, Bénédictine, Angostura bitters and Peychaud's bitters. Named after the French Quarter, this strong cocktail was reportedly invented at the Carousel bar in the 1930s.*

SideCar*- brandy, sugar, lemon, another French-American hybrid, the sidecar is said to be the child of an American army captain living in Paris during the First World War.*

Absinthe Frappe*- absinthe, mint soda, water and crushed ice a truly historic cocktail thats not as easy to find on New Orleans menus as it used to be. In 1912, the cocktail was banned when rumors circled that absinthe caused delirium and hallucinations.*

Cocktail de la Louisiane*- rye, sweet vermouth, Benedictine, Peychaud's bitters, and absinthe. Order the Sazerac's close , but lesser known cousin at a local bar and you'll sound like a real insider to the cocktail-world.*

6 **Cat's Meow** – ***E5*** – *701 Bourbon St. - ✆504 523 2788 - 701bourbon.com - 2pm-6am weekends; 4pm-6am Mon-Thur.* This rowdy karaoke bar, with a karaoke stage, four bars, and two floors, is open until dawn. It is a favorite for bachelor and bachelorette parties, and really anyone else who came to New Orleans to let loose and belt out their favorite songs.

4 **Carousel Bar** – ***D4*** – *214 Royal St., Hotel Monteleone - ✆504 523 3341 - www.hotelmonteleone.com - daily 11am-12am.* The bar room (off of the lobby at the Hotel Monteleone) centers around a slowly spinning bar top, gracefully adorned like an authentic carousel. There is often live jazz music, and (almost always) throngs of hotel guests and tourists enjoying brunch bloody marys and brandy milk punches, or evening French75 cocktails (gin or brandy, champagne, sugar and lemon).

6 **Chart Room** – ***E5*** – *300 Chartres St. - ✆504 522 1708- daily 11am-4am.* From the looks of it, you wouldn't believe this neighborhood dive makes some of the best sazeracs in the

area. Doors open out onto the street for delightful french quarter people watching. Cash only.

6 **Cosimo's** - ***E5*** - *1201 Burgundy St. - ✆504 522 9715 - daily 4pm-5am.* A friendly pool bar and neighborhood spot, you'll find more locals than tourists here. Cheap draft beers, pub snacks like pizza and fried green beans, and great street views during Mardi Gras, all make it worth finding the place.

6 **Erin Rose** - ***E5*** - *811 Conti St. - ✆504 522 3573 - www.erinrosebar.com - daily 10am-7am.* Among the indulgent draws to Erin Rose are the frozen Irish Coffees (like caffeinated milkshakes spiked with Jameson) and Killer Po' Boys served from a window in the back. Come with cash (no credit cards) and ready to shove your way through the crowds of locals and tourists.

6 **Golden Lantern** - ***E5*** - *1239 Royal St. - ✆504 529 2860 - 24/7.* Glowing paper lanterns adorn the ceiling at this otherwise humble corner barroom, which has been a staple in the neighborhood's gay community since the 1960s. It serves as a venue for many events during Southern Decadence, New Orlean's own gay pride festival over Labor Day weekend.

6 **Lafitte's Blacksmith Shop** - ***E5*** - *941 Bourbon St. - ✆504 593 9761 - www.lafittesblacksmithshop.com - daily 10am-3am.* It's just like New Orleans to turn a piece of history into a barroom. Part history, part legend says that this building once held the shop of the famous pirate Jean Lafitte. Built sometime between 1722 and 1732, it's one of the oldest buildings in the United States. Now it's a friendly piano bar on the quieter side of Bourbon Street (though not at all quiet inside) and an essential stop for any visitor making a barroom tour of the city.

6 **Molly's at the Market** - ***E5*** - *1107 Decatur St. - ✆504 525 5169 - www.mollysatthemarket.net - daily 10am-6am.* This friendly Irish pub makes a great Pimms cup, Irish Coffee, and Moscow Mule. Seating looks out onto the crowds of Decatur street, and local beers are offered on draft. There is usually a food pop-up in the back.

6 **Old Absinthe House** - ***E5*** - *240 Bourbon St. - ✆504 523 3181 - www.ruebourbon.com - daily 9am-3am (5am weekends).* Both a casual pit stop in the center of the Quarter and a great place to sample authentic absinthe.

6 **Pat O'Briens** - ***E5*** - *718 St Peter St. - ✆504 525 4823 - www.patobriens.com - Mon-Thur 12pm-2am; Fri-Sun 10am-4am.* While the hurricane cocktail has since been widely commercialized, the courtyard and barroom at Pat O'briens is still a fun place to enjoy the tall, pink cocktail invented here in the 1940s. Hurricane glasses, as well as the mix, are for purchase to take home.

6 **Napoleon House** - ***E5*** - *500 Chartres St. - Rivoli - ✆01 42 92 00 24 - www.napoleonhouse.com - daily 11am-2am; brunch Sun (26 €).* As the story goes, New Orleans Mayor Nicholas Girod proposed this corner building as the site of exile for ousted Emperor Napoleon Bonaparte around

1812. This plan never came to be, and the Impastato family has operated a bar and restuarant here since 1914. Famous for their Pimm's cups and exciting memoriabilia from over the decades, the interior's current day wear-and-tear only adds to its charm.

FAUBOURG MARIGNY AND BYWATER

***Area map* p. 45**

Cafés

1 Satsuma Cafe - ***F5*** - *3218 Dauphine St. - 504 304 5962 - www.satsumacafe.com - daily 7am-5pm.* This airy, artist's cafe offers coffee, fresh juices, healthy breakfasts and an outdoor patio.

Bars

71 Bacchanal - ***G4*** - *600 Poland Ave. - 504 948 9111 - www.bacchanalwine.com - daily 11am-12am.* Evolving from a tiny wine shop, a backyard, and a food truck, Bacchanal is now a full swing operation with upstairs seating, an outdoor stage, nightly choices of tapas, and beer, cocktails, and bottles of wine for purchase. Nightly live, local music under the twinkling outdoor lights makes this place irresistible. Go early or during the week for a chance at a prime table by the stage.

12 Friendly Bar - ***G5*** - *2301 Chartres St. - 504 943 8929 - daily 11am-3am.* An LGBTQ-friendly bar with cheap drinks, welcoming regulars and an ample dance floor, this is a great stop between the Marigny and the French Quarter.

14 Hi Ho Lounge - ***F5*** - *2239 Saint Claude Ave. - 504 945 4446 - www.hiholounge.net - 5pm-1am (4am Saturdays).* This dimly lit dive in the heart of St. Claude Ave. is known for its events (EP release parties, comedy showcases, Saturday night DJ sets), cheap pitchers of beer, and specialty french fries served in the courtyard out back.

22 Mimi's in the Marigny - ***G6*** - *2601 Royal St. - 504 872 9868 - daily 11am-4am.* A popular pre, post, and during parade spot for Mardi Gras, the crowd at Mimi's is local and festive. Downstairs, you'll find a dance floor,

Happy Hours

5 Bar Frances* - C3 - *4525 Freret St. - Uptown - 504 371 5043 - 4pm-7pm - $6 aperol spritz, sazerac and other cocktails. Whipped feta, warm olives, and other snacks.

92 St. Roch Market* - A4 - *2381 St Claude Ave. - Bywater - 504 609 3813 - 4pm-6pm - 75-cent oysters, $5 daiquiri, tom collins and sazerac cocktails. $5 wine glasses.

11 Domenica* - D3 - *123 Baronne St. - CBD - 504 648 6020 - 2pm-5pm - Half-off pizzas, beer, wine, and cocktails.

5 The Country Club* - C3 - *634 Louisa St. - Bywater - 504 945 0742 - 4pm-7pm (or any time it's raining!) - No, this gay-friendly bar and restaurant with a courtyard pool is not an actual country club. $3 well drinks, small plates specials.

pool table, and wide bar with plenty of room for making friends. Upstairs is a quiet wine bar with small tables, serving tapas and steak, ideal for a date or more intimate occasion.

9 **Parleaux Beer Lab** - ***G4*** - *634 Lesseps St. - ✆504 702 8433 - www.parleauxbeerlab.com - 3pm-10pm; closed Tues and Weds* . Besides churning out good brews, this small brewery attracts neighbors and visitors with its large backyard and seating area. Most nights of the week you'll find food trucks or pop-up kitchens out back, and a variety of events, from free yoga to trivia.

10 **Three Muses** - ***G4*** - *536 Frenchmen St. - ✆504 252 4801 - www.3musesnola.com - daily 5pm-11pm.* This intimate bar, restuarant, and music venue is among the classiest (and quietest) options on Frenchmen street. Put your name down for a table early, or look for a seat at the miniscule bar, and you'll be treated to two sets (most nights) of small piano or acoustic acts. The kitchen serves small plates, and the bar menu consists of well-selected wines and fresh craft cocktails.

72 **Siberia Lounge** - ***F5*** - *2227 St Claude Ave - ✆504 265 8855 - www.siberialounge.com - 4pm-2am.* Entertainment at this relaxed club ranges from DJ sets to comedy and burlesque. Thursday nights is the "Eastern Bloc Party" with contemporary Balkan bands. The kitchen serves "Slavic soul food" (think peirogis and blinis) from a window in the back.

CBD AND WAREHOUSE DISTRICT

Cafés

24 **Pulp and Grind** - ***F8*** - *644 Camp St. - ✆504 510 4037 - www.pulpandgrind.com - Tue-Sat 11.45am-6.30pm.* Enjoy fresh juices, pastries, and coffee in a relaxed evironment.

87 **Merchant** - ***E6*** - *800 Common St. - ✆504 571 9580 - www.merchantneworleans.com - daily 7am-5pm (closes 1pm Sat and Sun).* This sophisticated shop makes a great stop for coffee, breakfast sandwiches and crepes while exploring the CBD.

Bars

75 **Lucy's Retired Surf Bar** - ***EF7*** - *701 Tchoupitoulas St. - ✆504 523 8995 - www.lucysretiredsurfers.com - 11am-12am (2am Thu-Sat).* On a rowdy block in the otherwise quiet Warehouse District, this beach-themed bar serves Coronas and margaritas to large crowds after festivals, weddings, and events.

20 **Loa** - ***F7*** - *International House Hotel, 221 Camp St. - ✆504 553 9550 - www.ihhotel.com/loa - daily 4pm-1am.* It's possible for a quality craft cocktail bar to also be unpretentious, because it is so at Loa, a romantic hotel bar filled with Moroccan cushions, vintage pieces and rare liqueurs. Friendly barkeeps are happy to discuss spirits and their beloved city at all hours of the night.

21 **Cellardoor** - ***E7*** - *916 Lafayette St - ✆504 265 8392 - www.cellardoornola.com - 4pm-11pm (1am Fri and Sat; closed Sun).* From

the brick-walled bottom rooms of a historic 1830s home emerges this sophisticated cocktail bar and restaurant, perhaps the most romantic bar in the neighborhood. The kitchen serves small bites with international flavors.

75 **Sazerac Bar** - ***EF7*** - *The Roosevelt Hotel, 130 Roosevelt Way - ℘504 648 1200 - 11am-2am.* Gorgeous art deco murals, walnut fixtures, and leather chairs abound at the sexy sazerac bar inside the roosevelt hotel. Hands down, the best time to order a Ramos Gin Fizz is here, where famous Louisiana governor Huey P Long used to drink them. Regardless of what expertly crafted cocktails you order from the bowtied barkeep, it's one of the classiest places to drink in the city.

75 **Piscobar** - ***EF7*** - *Catahoula Hotel, 914 Union St. - ℘504 603- 2442 - 1pm-10pm (12am Fri and Sat).* The cocktail menu at this smart little hotel bar, with a fabulous inner courtyard, highlights the peruvian brandy pisco. Traditional pisco sours are great on a warm evening, and the bartenders always have a list of more inventive, sophisticated cocktails to choose from.

GARDEN DISTRICT

***Area map* p. 31**

Cafés

30 **French Truck Coffee** - ***D7*** - *1200 Magazine St. - ℘504 298 1115 - www.breadandroses.fr - daily 7am-6pm.* In this small shipping container, you can taste (and purchase to take home) coffee from one of the best small batch roasters in town. The shop also serves pastries and espresso drinks.

Bars

77 **Avenue Pub** - ***E6*** - *1732 St Charles Ave. - ℘504 586 9243 - www.theavenuepub.com - 24/7.* 24 hours and 7 days a week, you can enjoy hundreds of craft beers from this local pub with a serious penchant for good brew. The pub food menu includes hand cut french fries, chicken confit, and currywurst.

25 **Bakery Bar** - ***E5*** - *1179 Annunciation St. - ℘504 265 8884 - www.bakery.bar - 10am-12am; closed Mon.* Two delights reign at this unassuming corner spot by the 1-10 underpass: delicious cocktails and doberge cake, a specialty local dessert made from thin layers of cake and frosting. Add a great brunch menu and a happy hour of affordable martinis and snacks, and you can't go wrong at Bakery Bar.

27 **Barrelproof** - ***E6*** - *1201 Magazine St. - ℘504 299 1888 - www.barrelproofnola.com- daily 4pm-1am.* A dark barroom with a delicious kitchen and hip local crowd, Barrelproof specializes in whiskeys from all over the world.

6 **Half Moon** - ***E5*** - *1125 St Mary St. - ℘504 593 0011 - www.halfmoongrillnola.com - daily 12pm-4am.* A deliciously divey local bar (think ratty furniture, bad lighting, and drinks served in plastic), the back patio here is a nice spot to enjoy a casual drink while in the neighborhood.

(28) **Parasol's** – ***D6*** – *2533 Constance St. - ℘504 302 1543 - 11am-10pm.* The frozen Irish Coffees and pleasantly local crowd are the first draws to this local dive bar. But perhaps the best thing is the dingy-looking dining room through the back: here Parasol's kitchen serves some of the best roast beef and fried shrimp po boys (the firecracker shrimp is tossed in butter and hot sauce). If you're looking for a snack, try the irish sundae: potato salad drenched in roast beef gravy. It's a fun place to spend St. Patrick's day.

(31) **Tracey's** – ***D8*** – *2604 Magazine St. - ℘504 897 5413 - www.traceysnola.com - 11am-10pm (12am Fri and Sat).* Roast beef po boys at Tracey's rival those at the neighboring Parasol's, but the vibe here is somewhat different. The bar is large, with several TVs and a popular place for young, local crowd and older regulars to watch sports games. On many weekend nights, an oyster shucker sets up at a table outside Tracey's and sells fresh trays-full.

(76) **Delachaise** – ***E6*** – *3442 Saint Charles Ave. - ℘504 895 0858 - www.thedelachaise.com - Mon-Thu 5pm-2am; Fri-Sun 12pm-2am.* In a small building shaped like a streetcar, this wine bar offers 36 bottles "under $36", romantic seating on a wide patio under twinkling lights, and delicious moules frites and gastropub fare. It's a fantastic date spot.

UPTOWN

Cafes

(78) **Rue de la Course** – ***B5*** – *1140 S Carrollton Ave. - ℘504 861 4343 - www.ruedelacourse.com - daily 6:30am-11pm.* College students flock to Rue de la course for its late hours and ample study room. Others enjoy it for its gorgeous architecture, in a former bank building and with loads of natural light, good coffee and delicious pastries.

Bars

(33) **Dos Jefes** – ***C5*** – *5535 Tchoupitoulas St. - ℘504 891 8500 - www.dosjefes.com - daily 9am-7pm, 5pm-3am.* Perhaps the only place left in the city where you can smoke inside, this cigar bar offers a wide variety of commercial and harder-to-find smokes, Latin American rums, and cheap beer and wine. There is often live music, and pool in the back. It's a great spot for a date, or a festive night cap.

(79) **Kingpin** – ***E4*** – *1307 Lyons St. - ℘504 891 2373 - 3pm-2am.* This pleasant dive knows everyone in the neighborhood. Come for the people-watching and (often unoccupied) shuffleboard table in the corner. Most nights, a favorite local taco truck serves snaks out front.

(79) **Tchoup Yard** – ***E4*** – *405 Third St. - ℘504 895 6747 - www.tchoupyard.com - daily 11:30am-12am.* Someone's bright idea to turn this large industrial yard into a beer garden, with wine on tap, specialty frozen drinks, multiple food trucks each night, and lawn games. It's a great place for large groups.

MID CITY AND BAYOU ST. JOHN

Cafés

35 **Pagoda Cafe** - ***B4*** - *1430 N Dorgenois St. - ✆504 644 4178 - www.pagodacafe.net - 7:30am-3pm; Closed Mon.* Besides great coffee drinks and pleasant vibes, this popular, tiny spot in the Seventh Ward serves mango lassis, housemade sodas, pastries, sandwiches and great breakfast tacos. Park yourself on a picnic table outside and stay a while.

79 **The Station** - ***E4*** - *4400 Bienville St. - ✆504 309 4548 - daily 6:30am-8pm.* A neighborhood cafe with plenty of indoor and shaded outdoor seating. Offerings of sandwiches, quiches and inventive pastries, like the vegan "oreos" and savory kolaches, make it more inviting.

Bars

79 **Bayou Beer Garden** - ***E4*** - *326 N Jefferson Davis Pkwy - ✆504 302 9357 - www.bayoubeergarden.com - daily 11am-2am.* The backyard beer garden at this local's spot fills up quickly on weekends, and with good reason. There's a little something for everyone, with a wine bar and charcuterie spot adjoining a sportier beer yard that often crawfish boils in the spring.

6 **Finn McCool's** - ***E5*** - *3701 Banks St. - ✆504 486 9080 - www.finnmccools.com - Mon-Thu. 11am-2am; Fri-Sun 9am-3am.*To the delight of international soccer fans, this friendly Irish pub often opens early in the morning (and fills with fans) to stream European games. It's not a bad place to watch American football, either. Every year at St. Patrick's day, Finn's blocks off the whole street and throws an all-day party. After Hurricane Katrina, the generous owners and staff here provided a lot of support to the badly flooded neighborhood. Finn's still has a very loyal band of regulars.

34 **Pal's** - ***D3*** - *949 N Rendon St. - ✆504 488 7257 - daily 3pm-3am.* A neighborhood bar with good vibes and a lively scene. There is pool and air hockey in the back, and most nights of the week a food pop-up or free offerings out front. Specialty cocktails (like the Gingerita) and beer and shot specials are a good bet.

79 **Treo**- ***E4*** - *3835 Tulane Ave. - ✆504 304 4878 - treonola.com - daily 4pm-10pm.* Bartenders craft all the expert classics here (gin fizz, vieux carre, French75, and many more), served best during the happy hour when you can try them all for $6 each. A courtyard out back and upstairs gallery provide plenty of entertaining options. The kitchen serves crawfish, po boys, and fried seafood plates.

79 **Twelve Mile Limit** - ***E4*** - *500 S Telemachus St. - ✆504 488 8114 - daily 5pm-2am, opens 10am Sat and Sun* As divey as it looks, this bar actually has some of the best (and most affordable cocktails) in the city. Special entertainment includes monthly dance parties, weekly free dinner, and comedy night.

BREWERIES (CAN MAKE BOX)

Post Katrina renewal brought craft beer for the first time to New Orleans. Other than Abita Brewery (which isn't technically in New Orleans, nor technically "craft" anymore), NOLA brewery was the first in town making fresh, local beer. Since then, the scene has become much more crowded, to imbibers delight, and the stretch of Tchoupitolous Street, where you'll find NOLA and several others, previously a zone of old warehouses along the river on the way to the highway, has been rebranded as "beer row."

The Brewbus – (*www.nolabrew bus.com; 504 655 2153; starting at $65 per person*) leads several types of tours through the local breweries, with plenty of stops for beer drinking, of course.

Courtyard Brewery – ***E5*** – *1020 Erato St. - 504 522 3573 - www. courtyardbrewing.com - Wed 4pm-9:30pm; Thu-Sat 11am-10:30pm; Sun 11am- 9:30pm.* A small, hole-in-the-wall brewery with a pleasant courtyard (often hosting a food truck). This is the only place you can taste their beers.

79 **Port Orleans** – ***E4*** – *4124 Tchoupitoulas St. - 504 266 2332 - 11am-10pm; closed Tue.* Delicious brunch, one of the newest brewers in town just taking off.

6 **NOLA Brewery** – ***E5*** – *811 Conti St. - 504 522 3573 - www. erinrosebar.com - daily 10am-7am.* The oldest craft brewery with a well-established tap room.

6 **Urban South Brewery** – ***E5*** – *1645 Tchoupitoulas St. - 504 267 4852 - www.urbansouthbrewery.com - Mon-Wed 4pm-9pm; Thur-Sun 12am-9pm.* Large, kid friendly warehouse and delicious beers. Boils crawfish in large quantities during the spring.

Wayward Owl Brewing 3940 Thalia St. - **504 827 1646 -** *www. waywardowlbrewing.com - Tue-Fri 3pm-9pm; Sat and Sun 12pm-9pm - closed Mon.* Full of games, food trucks, and fun, this Mid City brewery makes a point to produce beers hard to find elsewhere in the city.

Broad Street Cider and Ale broadstreetcider.com - Tues. and Wed 4pm-9pm; Thur-Sat. 1pm-9pm. closed Sun and Mon. Cider drinker's delight in the Broadmoor area, where creative ciders and delicious ales are highlighted in a chic, casual setting.

Cajun Fire Brewing Company - *10555 Lake Forest Blvd - 504 355 6653 - www. drinkcajunfire.com -* The city's first Black-owned brewery makes seriously good beers that are well worth the trip out to New Orleans East.

Shopping

You will find the key shopping districts on the map p. 136-137.

Opening Hours: Shops typically open around 9pm until 6pm, though shops in busy sections of the French Quarter can stay open as late as 9pm to catch evening shoppers. Small boutiques tend to keep shorter hours, opening around 11 or 12 and closing at 5 or 6. Small shops are closed or keep shorter hours on Sundays.

CLASSIC SHOPPING

With the exception of the art galleries and boutiques on or around **Royal Street**, most shops in the French Quarter cater to tourists, selling Mardi Gras beads and masks, hot sauce, specialty food items and other trinkets. Shopping the Quarter is easily done by foot.

Magazine Street stretches from the CBD to Audubon Park, a six-mile stroll that can fulfill all your shopping needs. To shop Magazine Street, take the St. Charles Street car from the CBD or Uptown and walk the long shopping district. Alternatively, the #11 bus runs from Canal St. and Magazine through the entire length of Magazine Street.

Magazine Street

Your best bet is to purchase a $3.00 all day transit pass (includes bus and streetcar), so you can hop on and off the bus to window-shop at your leisure. The Magazine Street Merchants Association website (*www.magazinestreet.com*) provides a helpful guide of shops, sales, and events in the area.

LUXURY SHOPPING

The Shops at Canal Place (*333 Canal St.*), a luxury mall in the center of the CBD, has several chain luxury and high-end stores, including a **Saks Fifth Avenue** department store. Many high-end boutiques can be found on Magazine Street in the blocks toward Uptown and Audubon Park.

ANTIQUE SHOPPING

French Quarter: Royal Street, between St. Phillip and Iberville Sts., is home to a high concentration of quality antique shops.
Shop **Magazine Street**, between Napoleon and Washington Aves., for vintage and antique housing goods, art, and furniture.

ART SHOPPING

Royal Street and the surrounding area feature the most galleries in the French Quarter. Julia Street, in the Warehouse District, is known as the gallery district. On the first Saturday in August, local art organizations host White Linen Night, a festive wine-and-cheese walk through the gallery openings of the district.

TOURIST SHOPPING

Buy beads, masks, signs, food goods in the french quarter, especially near Canal, St. Peter, and Decatur Streets. Local vendors sell New Orleans-themed crafts and goods in **The French Market** (*700 Decatur St.*) every day from 10am to 6pm. Across from the French Market and Jackson Square, on St. Peter and Decatur Streets, find several shops for purchasing local treats and food goods.

TRENDY SHOPPING

Canal Street in the CBD features several jeans, sneaker and urban clothing stores. In the Lower Garden District section of Magazine Street you'll find funky clothing boutiques, secondhand and vintage stores catering to a young, hip crowd.

OUR PICKS

Fashion

1 Meyer the Hatter - ***D5*** - *120 St Charles Ave. - ✆504 525 1048 - 10am-5:45pm; closed Sun - meyerthehatter.com.* Since 1894 (and still run by generations of the same family) Meyer the Hatter has been here to please. The headware selection has diversified over the years, but their collection of felt Stetsons (with plumes and feathers for customizing) are among the best. The friendly owners won't let you go unassisted.

French Market

2 Defend New Orleans – ***F5*** – *1101 First St. - ✆504 941 7010 - 11am-6pm - www.dno.la.* T-shirts, hats, stickers, and jackets, with hip, unique designs, are emblazened with messages in support of (or inspired by) New Orleans. You'll notice locals wearing the iconic "Defend New Orleans" skull t-shirt after you purchase your own. A second store can be found inside the Ace Hotel building at 600 Carondolet St.

Local Specialties and Gifts

3 Faulkner House Books – ***E5*** – *624 Pirate Alley - ✆504 524 2940 - 10am-5:30pm - www.faulkner housebooks.com.* Inside a former home once rented by William Faulkner and where he wrote some of his earliest work, lies this peaceful literary oasis. Fellow bookworms sell contemporary literature, rare books and first editions, and of course, books by and about Faulkner.

Palace Art Market

At this nightime bazaar in the heart of Frenchmen Street's nightlife district, night owls can take a break between visitng neighboring music clubs to peruse local arts and crafts and chat with the friendly vendors. The open-air market operates 7 evenings a week at 619 Frenchmen St. (www. palaceartmarket.com).

4 Hove Parfumeur – ***F5*** – *434 Chartres St. - ✆504 525 7827 - 9:30am-6pm (opens 11am Sun).* Family generations at Hove have been helping individuals create their ideal fragrance from fine essential oils and perfumes since the 1930s. The shops sights, smells, and general ambiance still feel locked in time (a whimsical, feminine time).

5 Mignon Faget – ***G5*** – *3801 Magazine St. - ✆504 891 2005 - 10am-6pm - www.mignonfaget.com.* Since the 1970s, artist Mignon Faget's fine jewelry has paid subtle homage to the city of New Orleans. Pendants, bracelets, earrings and home goods feature fleur de lis, crawfish, honeycomb, crabs, alligators and other imagery of the Gulf South and Crescent City. You can also purchase her jewelry inside the Lakeside Shopping Center, shops at Canal Place, and the Outlets at the Riverwalk.

9 Tchoup Industries – ***E4*** – *1115 St Mary St. - ✆504 872 0726 - www.tchoupindustries.com - 11am-6pm (12am-5pm Saturdays); closed Wednesdays.* Sturdy bags (from wallets and medicine bags to backpacks and totes) support a sustainable future. Bags are often made from local and recycled materials like reused rice burlap, sail cloth, alligator skin and nutria fur.

Food

6 New Orleans School of Cooking and Louisiana General Store – ***G5*** – *524 St Louis St. - ✆800 237 4841 - 9am-6pm - www.store.nosoc.com.* Take-home specialty food goods like Cajun spice mix, olive salad for recreating your own muffalettas, chicory coffee, pralines and hot sauce. The store also sells cookbooks, cookware festive aprons and other kitchen gear.

Arts and Antiques

8 Rodrigue Studios – ***F4-5*** – *730 Royal St. - ✆504 581 4244 - www.georgerodrigue.com - 10am-6pm (12-5pm Sundays).* On a colorful corner of Royal Street, you'll spot Rodrigue's vibrant paintings, influenced by Cajun landscapes and often featuring a small blue dog. Louisiana native George Rodrigue's blue dog first originated in the 90s, inspired by Cajun folklore of the "loup-garu," and has become an iconic image around New Orleans, and in an international art scene, ever since. Rodrigue passed away in 2013 and his family still manages his collections and gallery space.

11 Secondline Arts and Antiques – ***G3*** – *1209 Decatur St. - ✆504 875 1924- Sun-Wed. 8am-8pm; Thurs. 8am-10pm; Fri and Sat. 8am-12am - www.secondlinenola.com.* Part flea market, part bazaar, part antique store, the rambling rooms of this building seem to go on forever, full of delights and eye candy, both historical and crafty. The shop also rents bicycles, and a stand in the courtyard sells snoballs during the hotter months.

Nightlife

The Big Easy is known for jubilant celebrations and wild entertainment. Most famous for its jazz, there are affordable ways to experience live, local music of this vibrant city around every corner.

Find the addresses on our maps using the numbers in the listings (ex. 1). The coordinates in red (ex. C2) refer to the detachable map (inside the cover).

THEATER

Broadway and large theatrical productions often come to the **Saenger Theater** *(1111 Canal St.; ℘504 525 1052; www.saengernola.com)* **The Joy Theater** *(1200 Canal St.; ℘504 528 9569; www.thejoytheater.com)*; **Mahalia Jackson Theater** *(1419 Basin St.; ℘504 525 1052; www.mahaliajacksontheater.com)*, and **Civic Theater** *(510 O'Keefe Ave; ℘504 272 0865; www.civicnola.com)*, host a series of large concerts and events. Check **The New Movement theater** *(2706 St Claude Ave.; ℘504 302 8264; www.comedynola.com)*, for improv, comedy and local indie productions.

BURLESQUE, DRAG AND CABARET

Weekends at the **AllWays Lounge** *(2240 St Claude Ave; ℘504 218 5778; www.theallwayslounge.net)* guarantee all three (as well as comedy, late night DJs, and affordable drinks). **Gravier Street Social** (*523 Gravier St.; ℘504 941 7629; www.gravierstreetsocial.com*) and **Burgundy Bar** (*at The Saint Hotel, 931 Canal St.; ℘504 522 5400; www.thesainthotelneworleans.com*), have regular weekend burlesque performances. Drag shows can be found throughout the French Quarter and the gay bars of Bourbon Street.

OPERA AND ORCHESTRA

The **Louisiana Philharmonic Orchestra** holds regular concerts at **The Orpheum Theater** (*129 Roosevelt Way*), and some special events at other venues around town. Check www.lpomusic.com for a full schedule.

9 **Marigny Opera House** – ***E3*** – *725 St. Ferdinand St. - ℘504 948 9998 - www.marignyoperahouse.org*. This dance and music venue utilizes the space and acoustics of a gorgeous 1850s Catholic church. Home to their own contemporary ballet company, the Marigny Opera Ballet, the venue also hosts dance, jazz, classical music, and other unique performances.

LIVE MUSIC

Some shows are free, but most clubs charge a small cover or have a drink minimum. Bring cash: many bands rely on tips to make ends meet, and tipping the band supports the future of live, local music in the city.

Wednesdays at the Square

Wednesdays during spring, locals gather to hear some of the very best bands around play free concerts, as part of a series benefiting the Youth Leadership Council. Local restaurants sell specialty food and drink out of stands set up around the square. Wednesday evenings - concerts from 5-7pm, Mid March thru Late May - Lafayette Square in the CBD (across from Gallier Hall and just off of St. Charles Ave.)

Before planning your night out, check the local radio station's Livewire, a comprehensive calendar of live music around town, at *www.wwoz.org*.

Our selection of music venues

2 **d.b.a.** – ***A2*** – *618 Frenchmen St. - ✆504 942 3731 - www.dba neworleans.com - daily 5pm-till (4pm Fri and Sat).* This Southern branch of the NYC staple is always a good time. The best acts around town book here often, like Little Freddie King, Walter Wolfman Washington, and the New Orleans Cottonmouth Kings. Buy tickets at the door.

3 **Howlin' Wolf** – ***G7*** – *907 S. Peters St. - ✆504 529 5844 - www. thehowlinwolf.com.* Hip-Hop, comedy, jazz and other contemporary acts grace the small stages of the main bar and back "den." A mural, showcasing music legends blended with contemporary talent, flanks the bar's exterior. Catch the Hot 8 Brass Band every Sunday ($15).

8 **Le Bon Temps Roule** – ***E3*** – *4801 Magazine St. - ✆504 895 8117 - lbtrnola.com - daily 11am-till.* The Soul Rebels play here every Thursday night at 11pm. Other local brass bands, pianists, and jazz trios grace themusic calendar other nights. The beer is always cold and food is served until late.

8 **Maison** – ***E3*** – *508 Frenchmen St. - ✆504 371 5543 - www.maison frenchmen.com. - 4pm-3am; Fri and Sat 1pm-4am.* There's a full calendar of the best popular jazz and brass bands around town, with early (1pm) shows on weekends, and music continuing well past midnight.

9 **Maple Leaf Bar** – ***E3*** – *8316 Oak St. - ✆504 866 9359 - www. mapleleafbar.com - 3pm-4am.* While far Uptown from the musical blocks of Frenchmen Street, it's worth piling in to this iconic bar room on Tuesday nights for Rebirth Brass Bands' standing show.

3 **One Eyed Jacks** – ***G7*** – *615 Toulouse St. - ✆504 569 8361 - www. oneeyedjacks.net.* This crimson-walled, velvety lounge with a round bar at its center (and another in the front waiting room) hosts touring artists, burlesque shows, lady's arm wrestling, and showcases of local musical acts (especially during Mardi Gras and festivals).

8 **Preservation Hall** – ***E3*** – *726 St. Peters St. - ✆504 522 2841 - www. preservationhall.com .* An iconic stop

Preservation Hall

on any music lover's tour, the band plays at 5, 6, 8, 9 and 10pm every night. You can stand in line before any show for a $20 (cash) ticket, or purchase one online ahead of time for guaranteed seating ($10-15 more).

9 **Spotted Cat** – ***E3*** – *623 Frenchmen St. - ✆504 943 3887 - www.spottedcatmusicclub.com - 2pm-2am.* Dilapidated and eclectic, from its building's crooked front facade to the piano in the bathroom, this club is always a good time. Acts feature the hottest in contemporary, nontraditional jazz. There is usually a 2pm set as well as the evening ones. No reservations and cash only.

10 **Rock N' Bowl** – ***EF3*** – *3016 S Carrollton Ave. - ✆504 861 1700 - www.rocknbowl.com - Mon-Thurs 11:30am-12am; Fri and Sat. 11:30am-2am; closed Sun.* This bowling alley is also a bar, restaurant, and music venue, with a wooden stage and dance floor reminiscent of a Cajun dance hall. It's a great place to hear zydeco and Cajun music.

12 **Tipitina's** – ***H6*** – *501 Napoleon Ave. - ✆504 895 8477 - www.tipitinas.com.* Since 1977, Tipitina's has been a favorite venue to catch local music or national acts. There is Cajun dancing every Sunday afternoon.

Where to stay

Hotels in the French Quarter and CBD are walking distance from most sights, restaurants and streetcar lines. If you're looking for a quieter stay or alternative experience, consider booking in the Marigny, close to the nightlife and music clubs of Frenchmen Street; Mid City, a mostly residential neighborhood near City Park and many festivals, or the Lower Garden District, among the mansions and live oaks of gorgeous St. Charles Avenue.

Find the addresses on the detachable map (inside the cover) using the numbers included in the listings (ex. 1). The coordiantes in red (ex. D2) refer to the same map.

Our price ranges are established on the basis of one night in a standard double in low/high season. You may also find special promotional prices

FRENCH QUARTER

From $150 to $200

1 **Dauphine Orleans** - ***E5*** - *415 Dauphine St. - ✆504 586 1800 - www.dauphineorleans.com -* P *- 111 rooms.* This lovely, well-run hotel sits in a prime French Quarter location just steps from historic attractions. Choose a room in the main hotel or in the historic Hermann House; the latter boast jacuzzis and upgraded amenities. Continental breakfast is included along with afternoon snacks, and the courtyard pool is the perfect place to cool off after a day of sightseeing.

From $250 to $300

3 **Hotel Monteleone** - ***E4*** - *214 Royal St. - ✆504 523 3341 - www.hotelmonteleone.com - 600 rooms.* This historic hotel, an former favorite of Tennessee Williams and Truman Capote, hosts more bridal parties and conferences than literary figures these days, but the walls still drip with charm. The Carousel Bar, with its opulent, slow-spinning bartop, is the hotel's best feature, and a great place for a brunch mimosa or a jazz-filled cocktail hour.

4 **Omni Royal Orleans** - ***G4*** - *621 St Louis St. - ✆504 529 5333 - www.omnihotels.com - 345 rooms.* This historic corner once hosted some of the first Mardi Gras balls in history. While the original building has since been replaced, the Omni Royal of today is an elegant replica, and both the hotel and this block of the French Quarter maintain much of their early charm. Guests enjoy vaulted ceilings, refined rooms, marble lobbies, fine dining, and a French Riviera-inspired pool deck with views of the Quarter.

2 **Royal Sonesta Hotel** - ***F5*** - *300 Bourbon St. - ✆504 586 0300 - www.sonesta.com - 482 rooms.* For those seeking comfortable quarters right in the thick of things, select rooms at this hotel offer balconies overlooking Bourbon Street, with an

option for quieter rooms in the back, a serene inner pool deck, outdoor bar, and courtyard. Dining options include the Desire oyster bar, with fresh gulf oysters and pub food, or renowned luxury dining at Restaurant R'evolution.

4 **Soniat House** - ***G4*** - *1133 Chartres St. - ℘504 522 0570 - www.soniathouse.com - 30 rooms.* A short walk from Cafe du Monde, this classic Creole-style town house in the French Quarter hasn't changed much since its beginnings in 1930. Spiral staircases lead to rooms decorated with European and Louisiana antiques and hand-carved canopy beds, leading out to flower-filled balconies. Comfortable guest rooms feature luxurious amenities like bathrobes, Molton Brown products, Egyptian cotton bed linens and goosedown pillows.

CBD AND WAREHOUSE DISTRICT

From $150 to $180

16 **Catahoula Hotel** - ***F8*** - *914 Union St. - ℘504 603 2442 - www.catahoulahotel.com - 35 rooms - Breakfast 12 €.* Elegant and peaceful, this boutique hotel juxtaposes its hectic downtown surroundings. In the lobby, order espresso drinks, or pisco cocktails and Peruvian snacks from the black-and-white tiled bar. Enjoy the outdoors in the courtyard, where a larger than life female figured-mural watches over you, or on the rooftop patio for sunset views. Rooms are minimalist yet refined.

8 **International House Hotel** - ***C7*** - *221 Camp St. - ℘504 264 9079 - www.ihhotel.com - 117 rooms.* This small hotel offers standard, modern rooms, an excellent bar, and small but well-equipped gym. Look for hallways of musical tributes and modern art installations, lobby chess games, and one of the most romantic bars in the city. The Lobby decks itself out several times a year for its "rituals," seasonal, artistic events inspired by the city's Catholic and voodoo cultures.

From $200 to $250

8 **The NOPSI Hotel** - ***C7*** - *317 Baronne St. - ℘844 439 1463 - www.nopsihotel.com - 217 rooms.* This hotel opened in 2017 inside a former utilities building, and features vaulted ceilings and large suites. There is a rooftop pool, lobby bar, and restaurant. Rooms have modern bathrooms and loads of natural light.

From $250 to $300

5 **Ace Hotel New Orleans** - ***F7*** - *600 Carondelet St. - ℘504 900 1180 - www.acehotel.com/neworleans - 234 rooms.* With its in-house music venue, art installations, boutique shops from local vendors, seafood restaurant, and a rooftop pool resort, a visit to the Ace is more of a cultural experience rather than a typical hotel stay. The rooftop pool club is a place to see-and-be-seen while sipping tropical cocktails.

8 **Roosevelt Hotel** - ***C7*** - *123 Baronne St. - ℘504 648 1200 - www.therooseveltneworleans.com - 504 rooms.* This hotel has tons of history, but, thanks to a complete renovation,

The Drifter Hotel

tons of comfort, too. The grand dame days can still be remembered in the chandeliered marble lobby (especially around Christmas time, when the halls are decked) or in the walnut-paneled Sazerac Bar.

Over $300

Windsor Court Hotel – ***Off map C8*** – *300 Gravier St. - ✆504 523 6000 - www.windsorcourthotel.com - 316 rooms.* Frequented by European royalty and celebrities, this opulent hotel on the outskirts of the French Quarter received a complete interior renovation in 2012. Guest rooms and suites are outfitted with fine linens (note the custom toile depicting New Orleans landmarks), flat-screen TVs and elegant furnishings. High tea is served (Thu–Sun) in the lobby's Le Salon lounge.

THE MARIGNY

From $150 to $200

8 **Frenchmen Hotel** – ***C7*** – *417 Frenchmen St. - ✆504 945 5453 - www.frenchmenhotel.com - 27 rooms - Breakfast Included.* A casual, affordable inn lands you just steps from Frenchmen Street, the best place for live music in the city. Rooms are well maintained, most overlooking the inner courtyard and pool. It's a great choice for music lovers who don't mind late nights (noise from the street carries some). Complimentary breakfast is served in the courtyard each morning.

(8) **Melrose Mansion** - ***C7*** - *937 Esplanade Ave. - ✆504 944 2255 - www.melrosemansion.com - 21 rooms. - Continental Breakfast.* This renovated mansion is on a quiet section of Esplanade Ave., but an easy walking distance to both the Quarter and nightlife section of the Marigny neighborhoods. In the courtyard, you'll find one of the largest pools in the city. Minimalist rooms with large mirrors and modern furniture accent the room's original features, like high ceilings, wood floors, and original fireplaces.

LOWER GARDEN DISTRICT

Under $75

(12) **The Quisby** - ***E2*** - *1225 St. Charles Ave. - ✆504 208 4881 - www.thequisby.com - 30 rooms - Free Continental Breakfast.* A clean, modern hostel with hip features like the industrial bar and lobby, millennial-pink personal lockers, muraled hallways and bespoke bunk beds.

From $199 to $250

(12) **Henry Howard Hotel** - ***E2*** - *2041 Prytania St. - ✆504 313 1577 - www.henryhowardhotel.com - 18 rooms.* A historic mansion (named for Louisiana's renowned 19th Century architect) is a pleasant mixture of contemporary comforts and historic charm. Rooms have canopy beds, festive wallpaper, large windows, and select balconies. Check in takes place in the "parlor," where you'll also enjoy a welcome drink, coffee and water, and peruse historic mardi gras artifacts and books.

(12) **Pontchartrain Hotel** - ***E2*** - *2031 St Charles Ave. - ✆800 708 6652 - www.thepontchartrainhotel.com - 106 rooms.* Quite larger than other choices in the neighborhood, this renovated 1930s hotel comes with loads of style and cute nods to the building's (and the city's) past. There's a lobby sports bar and cafe, fine dining room, but the real star is Hot Tin, a festive rooftop bar with prohibition-style feel and unprecedented views of the city.

MID CITY AND BAYOU ST. JOHN

Around $199

(13) **Edgar Degas House** - ***F3*** - *2306 Esplanade Ave. - ✆504 821 5009 - www.degashouse.com - 9 rooms - Creole Breakfast $35.* On a gorgeous block of esplanade, this inn offers various-sized rooms with antique furniture and views of the garden and courtyard, where you'll enjoy a fantastic creole brunch, or evening cocktail under the twinkling lights. The french impressionist lived here while visiting his creole family, and his grand-nieces still run the inn, and a small museum within the house.

(19) **The Drifter Hotel** - ***F3*** - *3522 Tulane Ave. - ✆504 605 4644 - www.thedrifterhotel.com - 20 rooms.* A renovated 50s-style motel maintains its charm and kitsch, with upgrades like imported mexican tiles in every room, Casper mattresses, a heated pool and full calendar of entertainment under the courtyard's disco ball.

RTA
ST. CHARL
HOW'S MY DRIVING
CALL 248-3900
95
Please Have Exact Far
Or RTA Pass Ready

Find Out More

Streetcar, St. Charles Avenue

New Orleans cuisine

Rooted in traditions more than two centuries old, New Orleans cuisine reveals the divergent influences of the varied cultures who populated the city.

Cajun vs. Creole

The terms Cajun and Creole are applied to New Orleans' dishes so often that they might seem interchangeable. In fact, the two styles of cooking have quite different origins and flavors. Of course, over the years and with similar ingredients, livestock, and produce as their resources, the two share some similar (if not competing) dishes.

The origins of Cajun cooking lie in the simple foodways of agrarian France, brought to Louisiana by Acadian farmers and adapted with local ingredients. Considered more complex, Creole cuisine began in New Orleans and was influenced by the culinary traditions of the city's Spanish, African, West Indian and Native American populations.

Dependent as they are on the use of fresh local ingredients, many Cajun and Creole specialties are difficult to duplicate outside the region, making eating out, for some visitors, the raison d'être of a visit to the "Big Easy."

Gulf Flavors

Fish and seafood drawn from Louisiana rivers, lakes, brackish coastal wetlands and the Gulf of Mexico headline many a menu, accompanied by mellow Creole tomatoes, okra, red beans and other fruits and vegetables distinctive to the region's soil and climate. Complex combinations of herbs and spices spike many dishes. Roux, a mixture of flour and fat cooked until dark brown, forms the base of sauces and soups. These include gumbo, a rich stew typically made with okra, andouille (a spicy smoked pork sausage) and chicken or seafood, and thickened with filé (powdered sassafrass, first used by the region's Choctaw Indians).

Shellfish

Shrimp, oysters and crawfish (a freshwater shellfish resembling a miniature lobster) appear in countless forms: étouffée, or "smothered," in rich, vegetable-laced sauce;

Gumbo

simmered with rice, tomato, meats and spices in jambalaya; chilled and dressed with piquant rémoulade sauce; or dusted with cornmeal, then fried and heaped on French bread in a po' boy sandwich.

While you can find many quality raw Gulf oysters at New Orleans'restaurants, the preferred method of consuming them is char-grilled (also called char-boiled). This method traditionally uses a char grill or broiler to lightly bake the oysters on the half shell. Before cooking, oysters are doused in butter, parmesan, garlic, parsely, and breadcrumbs.

Each spring, crawfish season is a special time in Lousiana, with massive pots of mudbugs boiling in every resturant's kitchen, backyard, courtyard, and park. The small crustaceans are best served fresh, after being boiled in Cajun spices and often accompanied with boiled onions, potatoes, sausage and corn. When visiting in spring, keep an ear to the ground for work of the closest crawfish boil. If you aren't lucky enough to be invited to one by a local, many bars, restuarants, and breweries host them from the end of February well until May You can also pick up a sack to-go from any neighborhood seafood store.

Fresh Gulf Catches

Amberjack, redfish, pompano and trout are all fished locally and served up sautéed with almonds, napped with meunière sauce, or broiled and topped with sweet lump crabmeat.

Char-boiled oysters

For Dessert

New Orleanians love sweets, and there are many desserts to indulge in past the beignets. One local craze is the sno ball, cups of shaved ice, sometimes cream-filled, and drenched in syrups of different flavors. Sno ball stands operate seasonally, and one of the joyous signs of the beginning of spring are the crowds of people lining up outside their favorite neighborhood sno ball stand once it has opened for the season.

Bread pudding has its own New Orleans recipe, drenched in syrup, and is served at most Creole restaurants (don't miss it at Commander's Palace, where this decadent dessert must be ordered 45 minutes ahead of time). Try bananas Foster, a decadent preparation of bananas sautéed in butter and brown sugar then flamed with rum at table and served over ice cream.

Mardi Gras

New Orleans' Mardi Gras celebration is world-renowned as an unabashed invitation and tribute to escapism, ribaldry and decadence, a final hurrah before the spartan, sober season of Lent. The day before Ash Wednesday, Mardi Gras crowns the Carnival season, which officially begins on Twelfth Night (January 6). This season of parties, private mask and parades organized by exclusive social clubs known as "krewes" reaches its crescendo during the week and a half before Mardi Gras, during which time some 60 parades roll along established routes through various parts of the city. Costumed riders aboard elaborately designed floats, toss strings of beads, aluminum doubloons, plastic cups, toys and other trinkets to the crowds who line the streets begging for handouts. On Fat Tuesday itself, businesses and services shut down as residents and visitors alike take to the streets for a day-long citywide binge. Families dressed in costumes or in the Mardi Gras colors of purple, green and gold congregate along the St. Charles Avenue parade route to try for the

prized coconuts handed out by the members of the Zulu Social Aid and Pleasure Club; or to toast Rex, King of Carnival, as he passes by with the Krewe of Rex. Die-hard revelers don costumes and head for the French Quarter to pack themselves like sardines into the throngs of people on Bourbon Street. Here they gape at the outrageous creations of costume-contest participants, drink and dance, and indulge in New Orleans' quintessential celebration of escape from life's worries to focus on the pleasures of today.

Mardi Gras participants

Mardi Gras

STEAMER
NATCHEZ
PORT OF NEW ORLEANS
NATCHEZ.

Planning Your Trip

Steamboat Natchez

Know before you go

BY PLANE

Louis Armstrong Airport is a small airport, with plans to complete a second terminal (and general aiport expansion) in 2019. While technically an international airport, most international flights connect in Charlotte, Atlanta, or Miami.
Louis Armstrong International Airport (MSY)- 900 Airport Dr., Kenner, LA - 504 464 0831 - www.flymsy.com.

BY CAR

1-10 is usually the easiest way in and out of New Orleans, in either direction.
Parking in the French Quarter is near impossible, and hotels charge high rates (around $40) for valet (same goes for hotels in the CBD and Warehouse district). If staying in these neighborhoods, your best bet is to use a second-party parking lot or garage in the CBD. The CBD and Warehouse District have some limited parking, but be on the lookout for ruthless meter maids and follow all parking signage. Parking elsewhere in the city is quite easy.

BY BUS

The bus station is located in the CBD at 1001 Loyola Ave. (t*504 524 7571*) Greyhound buses connect New Orleans to the rest of the country; Megabus has routes to and from other major Southern cities.
Greyhound - *www.greyhound.com call 24/7, ℘1 800 231 2222; ℘214 849 8100 (international calls).*
Megabus - *www.megabus.com cal 24/7, ℘877 462 6342.*

BY TRAIN

Several Amtrak train lines connect New Orleans to the rest of the country in three routes:

The City of New Orleans (from Chicago, Memphis); **The Crescent** (from New York, Atlanta); and **the Sunset Limited** (from Los Angeles, Phoenix, Tucson, San Antonio).

The **Union Passenger Terminal** *(1001 Loyola Ave. - 800 872 7245)* is located in the CBD. Visit *www.Amtrak.com* to purchase tickets.

WHEN TO GO

Summer is the lowest season in New Orleans, especially from July to Mid September. During summer, temperatures can rise (and remain) in the mid-90s with incredibly high, oppressive humidity. That said, the city is well air-conditioned, many hotels have swimming pools, and the city is considerably less crowded during summer months. Airfare usually drops during this time, and many 4-star hotels offer lower, incentivizing rates, making many

SOME PRICE IDEAS FOR BUDGETING	
SERVICES OR ITEMS	**PRICE IN DOLLARS**
Single room in a budget hotel	79-99
A double room in a comfortable hotel	175-210
A double room in a superior category hotel	250-300
A meal in a simple restaurant	15-20 per person
A meal in a quality restaurant	25-45 per person
A meal in a gourmet restaurant	75-100 per person
A glass of wine	7-10
A cocktail in a bar	6-11
Entry to a museum	8.50-12
A single bus or streetcar ticket/5-day pass	1.25/15.00

top-notch rooms available for $100 or less.

Fall sees a rise in tourism in New Orleans, with the beginning of football season and many festivals from September thru November. Temperature and humidity stays high until October, when it usually drops to a tolerable 80 degrees. More affordable than the busy season of spring (with Mardi Gras and Jazz Fest spiking prices), this can be a great season to visit.

Winter temperatures in New Orleans tend to stay very mild, and even during the harshest winter, the city rarely experiences a freeze. In December and January, the city, decked out in holiday lights, entices visitors with Revillion dinners (prix-fixe, multi-course Creole meals at the finest restaurants) and Papa Noel rates at hotels (discounted Holiday season prices on rooms).

Spring is by far the busiest season in New Orleans. The weather goes from balmy, in February, to full-on hot by mid March, and Mardi Gras and many other festivals allure visitors from all over. Around Mardi Gras, Jazz Fest, and other events, expect airfare and hotel rates to double.

INFORMATION

Visitors: City of New Orleans - www.nola.gov/visitors
New Orleans Official Tourism Website - *www.neworleans.com*

BUDGET

Use the table above to help you set your budget.

Basic information

ACTIVITIES FOR KIDS

From swamp creatures to Mardi Gras, New Orleans can be a great destination for children. Don't forget these fun-filled spots:

- Audubon Zoo
- Audubon Insectarium
- Audubon Aquarium
- Louisiana Childrens Museum
- Mardi Gras World
- Barataria Preserve
- City Park

CYCLING

Thanks to new bike paths popping up all over the city, bicycling has become a fun and efficient way to get around the relatively small city of New Orleans.

Blue Bikes

Blue Bikes New Orleans (www. bluebikesnola.com) is a citywide bike share that allows you to rent a bike from a designated hub by swiping your credit card, and return it to any other hub around town. Pay hourly ($8/hour) or for the month ($15/hour, one hour of ride time per day).

Bike rental

If you plan to ride around town a lot, it's more cost effective to rent from a shop. Bikes usually include a helmet and lock.

Bicycle Micheals
622 Frenchmen St. - ✆504 945 9505 - www.bicyclemichaels.com.

Alex's Bikes *607 Marigny St - ✆504 327 9248 - www.alexsbikes.com.*

American Bicycle Rental Company
318 N Rampart St - 504 324 8257 - www.bikerentalneworleans.com.

Bike-taxi

Bike taxis are a fun, alternative way to get around. Most pedicabs operate in the French Quarter and areas of the CBD/Warehouse District.

NOLA Pedicabs *✆504 274-1300 www.nolapedicabs.com*

Bike Taxis Unlimited *✆504-891-3441 - www.neworleansbiketaxi.com.*

ACCESSIBILITY

In this guide, the ♿ symbol indicates sites that are accessible to people with reduced mobility.

Transport - All bus routes are wheelchair accessible, with retractable ramps, as are and Streetcar lines are except for certain historic St. Charles Ave. Streetcars (the GREEN streetcars; all RED streetcars are fully accessible). The RTA has plans to make all streetcars fully equipped with ramps. The Ferry and Ferry Terminal (visit the lower ramp to board). Louis Armstrong Airport is fully accessible.

United Cabs (*✆504 434 5700*) have wheelchair-accessible rides. **Uber Assist** rides include drivers able to assist riders, and can accomodate folding wheelchairs, but these

vehicles do not have ramps.
Lyft offers a similar service

Sights and Restaurants – *Access-louisiana.org* has a web application that can help you search which restaurants and sights are fully ADA accessible. Major museums and sights are fully accessible. Most restaurants and bars have made efforts to become accessible, even the oldest of buildings.

EMERGENCIES

Always dial 911 in an emergency.

HEALTH

Pharmacies open 24hr/24 and 7/7

Walgreens Pharmacy - *900 Canal St. - ℘504 568-1271*
Walgreens Pharmacy - *1801 St. Charles Ave. - ℘504 561 8458.*

NIGHTLIFE

Visit *www.wwoz.org/calendar/livewire-music* for listing of live music around town. Most jazz clubs pay a small cover or require a drink minimum. Always bring small bills for tipping the band. Most clubs will not allow children, even for afternoon shows. The Frenchmarket, jazz brunches, and the musical outdoor performances around Jackson Square or outdoor festivals are a good way to experience music with kids.

PUBLIC TRANSPORT

The streetcar, especially on St. Charles Avenue, is by far the most charming way to travel through New Orleans, but buses are fairly reliable, cheap, and can take you much farther throughout the city. Bus and Streetcar cost $1.25 for a single ride. The ferry cost two dollars (exact change, cash-only) each way. Bikes are allowed on all buses (on a front rack; only two bikes at a time) and on the ferry. Bikes are not allowed on the streetcar.

Streetcar

Streetcars typically operate every fifteen minutes. Visit *www.norta.com* for full schedules and routes. Most streetcar stops have a texting feature (with instructions) to learn when the next car will arrive)

#12 St. Charles Streetcar - from Canal St. at Carondolet St. (Warehouse District) to S. Carrollton at S. Claiborne (Uptown)

#2 Riverfront Streetcar - French Market Station (French Quarter) to Julia Street (Warehouse District)

#47 Canal St-Cemeteries - Harrah's Casino (CBD) to Canal at the Cemeteries (Mid City/Lakeview)

#48 Canal St-City Park - Harrah's Casino (CBD) to NOMA in City Park

#49 Rampart St. - St. Claude Union Passenger Terminal (Howard Ave./CBD) to St. Claude Ave. at Elysian Fields.

Bus
Buslines connect virtually every neighborhood in New Orleans, including Louis Armstrong Airport and neighborhoods on the West Bank of the Mississippi. Visit *www.norta.com* for full routes and schedules.

Ferry
The Algiers Point Ferry departs every half hour, on the quarter and three-quarter hour on the East (New Orleans) side, and on the half hour on the West Bank (Algiers) side. The ferry departs from a Canal Street Terminal close to Harrah's Casino and drops riders along the levee in Downtown Algiers Point.

Tourist offers

One day ($3), 3-day ($9) or 5-day ($15) Jazzy Passes are available on board or online ahead of time. The Algiers Ferry is not included in Jazzy Passes. Visit **www.norta.com**.

SAFETY

New Orleans has a reputation as a city with high crime, though crime has greatly improved in recent years. The French Quarter is perhaps the most policed area in the city, and violent crime rarely affects tourists. That said, exercise caution and common sense as you would in any urban area. Be cautious when walking alone or at night, especially in less populated or well lit areas. In the French Quarter or busy nightlife areas, keep your wits about you late at night: pickpockets and petty thieves sometimes look to target tourists that seem especially heavily intoxicated.

TAXIS

Where to find a taxi
You can easily hail a taxi in the French Quarter or CBD. Taxis line up outside of Harrah's Casino by Canal St. Uber and Lyft are fully operational services within New Orleans (require you to download their app on your Smartphone).

Taxis
United Cabs - *504 522-9771* or *504 524-9606 - www.unitedcabs.com*
New Orleans Carriage Cab Co. - *504 207 7777 - www.neworleanscarriagecab.com*

GUIDED TOURS

Walking tours
New Orleans Legendary Walking Tours - *www.neworleanslegendarywalkingtours.com*
Historic New Orleans Tours - *www.tourneworleans.com*

Bus tours
Grayline Tours - *www.graylineneworleans.com*

City Sightseeing Hop On Hop Off - *www.citysightseeingneworleans.com*

Cemetery Tours
Save Our Cemeteries - *www.saveourcemeteries.org*

Ghost Tours
Haunted History Tour - *(www.hauntedhistorytours.com)*

Voodoo Tours
Voodoo Bone Lady Tours - *www.voodooboneladytours.com hauntedhistorytours.com)*

Architectural Tours
New Orleans Architectural Tours - *www.nolatours.com*

Cocktail Tour
Grayline - *www.graylineneworleans.com/all/tours/cocktail-tour*

Brewery Tour
Nola Brewbus - *www.nolabrewbus.com*

Carriage Tours
Royal Carriages *(French Quarter) 700 Decatur St (at Jackson Square) - New Orleans, LA 70119 - ℘(504) 943-8820 - www.neworleanscarriages.com*

Canoe and Kayak
Companies around town rent kayaks or canoes for use on Bayou St. John or in City Park, and lead boat tours through several nearby swamps:

Kayakitiyak - *3494 Esplanade Ave. - ℘985 778 5034 - www.kayakitiyat.com.*

Canoe and Trail Adventures - *℘504 233-0686 - canoeandtrail.com.*

Riverboat Tours
Steamboat Natchez - *600 Decatur S treet, Suite 308 (Toulouse Street Wharf) - ℘504 569-1401 - www.steamboatnatchez.com - $34-83.* Daytime and Evening Jazz cruises with brunch and dinner options.

Creole Queen - *Outlet Collection at Riverwalk, 1 Poydras St. - ℘800 445 4109 - www.creolequeen.com - $30-80.* Historic or jazz cruises and special-themed holiday cruises, day and evening.

Airboat Tours
This has become a popular way to experience the swamp. Book a tour at one of the kiosks towards the bottom of Canal St., or book ahead of time with one of these companies. Tour boats operate outside of town, but often offer free bus service to their facility:

Airboat Adventures - *5145 Fleming Park Rd., Lafitte, LA - ℘504 689 2005; ℘888 467 9267 www.airboatadventures.com*

Jean Lafitte Swamp and Airboat Tours - *6601 Leo Kerner Pkwy., Marrero, LA - ℘504 587 1719; ℘800 445 4109 - www.jeanlafitteswamptour.com*

Flagship Private Tours - *6570 1/2 Louis XIV St., New Orleans, LA - ℘504 486 4562*

Swamp Adventures - *1265 Highway 3127, Hahnville, LA - ℘504 810-3866- www.aswampadventure.com*

TOURIST OFFICES

Louisiana Welcome Center - *529 St Ann St - ℘504 568 5661 - 8:30am-5pm*

Jean Lafitte National Historic Park and Preserve French Quarter Visitor Center - *419 Decatur St - ℘504 589 3882 - 9am-4:30pm; closed Sun and Mon.*

Festivals and events

New Orleans likes to boast that it's the festival capital of the world, and with good reason: the city knows how to throw a party. For a full calendar of festivals, visit www.neworleans.com

August-September 2018

▶**Satchmo Fest** – Aug 3-5 2018 - French Quarter - www.satchmo summerfest.orgr

▶**Whitney White Linen Night** – Aug 4 - Julia Street - www.cacno.org

© Paul Broussard/New Orleans Convention and Visitors Bureau

Red Dress Run

▶**Red Dress Run** – Aug 11 - Begins in Crescent Park - www.noh3.com

▶**Dirty Linen Night** – Aug 12 - 200-100 Royal Street - www.dirtylinennola.com

▶**Mid Summer Mardi Gras** – Last weekend in Aug - Oak Street -

▶**Southern Decadence** – Aug 30-Sept 3 - French Quarter - www.southerndecadence.net

▶**NOLA on Tap** – Sept 22 - City Park Festival Grounds - www. nolaontap.org

▶**Gretna Heritage Festival** – Sept 28-30 - Gretna, LA (Across the river) - www.gretnafest.com

October-November 2018

▶**Crescent City Blues and BBQ Festival** – Oct 12-14 - Lafayette Square - www.jazzandheritage.org/ blues-fest

▶**Krewe of Boo Parade** – Oct 20 - French Quarter - www.kreweofboo.com

▶**Voodoo Music and Arts Experience** – Oct 26-28 - City Park Festival Grounds - www.voodoo festival.com

▶**Halloween** – Oct 31 - Citywide.

▶**Treme Creole Gumbo Festival** – Second weekend in Nov - Congo Square - www.jazzand heritage.org/treme-gumbo/

Krewe of Boo Parade

PARK
CHICO'S

Jazz and Heritage Festival

December 2018-January 2019

▶**Celebration in the Oaks** – Nov 24, 2018-Jan 1, 2019 - City Park - www.neworleanscitypark.com/celebration-in-the-oaks

▶**Reviellion** – Month of Dec 2018 - Participating restuarants throughout the city - www.frenchquarter.com/reveillon-dinners

▶**Dick Clark's Rockin' New Years Eve** – Dec 31 - Jax Brewery - www.abc.go.com/shows/new-years-rockin-eve

February/March 2019

▶**Krewe du Vieux Parade** – Feb 16 - French Quarter and Marigny - www.kreweduvieux.org

▶**Chewbacchus Parade** – Feb 23- French Quarter and Marigny - www.chewbacchus.org

▶**Krewe of Nyx Parade** – Feb 27- Uptown - www.kreweofnyx.org

▶**Krewe of Muses Parade** – Feb 28- Uptown - www.kreweofmuses.org

▶**Krewe of Endymion** - https://endymion.org

▶**Krewe of Thoth** – thothkrewe.com

▶**Krewe of Bacchus** - www.kreweofbacchus.org
▶**Lundi Gras** – early March
▶**Mardi Gras Day** (Zulu and Rex parades) - Mar 5
▶**St. Patricks Day Parade** – Mar 17
▶**Buku Music and Arts Festival** – Mar 8-9 - thebukuproject.com
▶**Tennessee Williams Literary Festival** – late March
▶**Hogs for the Cause** – late Mar - www.hogsforthecause.org
▶**Wednesdays in the Square** – Mar-May

April 2019

▶**French Quarter Festival** – Apr 11-14 - French Quarter -fqfi.org
▶**Jazz and Heritage festival** (first weekend) – Apr 26-28 - Fairgrounds - www.jazzandheritage.org
▶**Festival International** (Lafayette) – late Apr - festivalinternational.org

May 2019

▶**Jazz and Heritage festival** (second weekend)–May 2-5 - Fairgrounds - www.jazzandheritage.org
▶**Bayou Boogaloo** – third weekend in May - Bayou St. John - www.thebayouboogaloo.com
▶**Greek Fest** – third weekend in May - 1200 Robert E Lee Blvd. - www.greekfestnola.com
▶**Treme/7th Ward Arts and Cultural Festival** – third weekend in May - Treme, under the Claiborne Ave. Bridge - www.treme7thwardcd.org
▶**Bayou Country Superfest** – late May - www.bayoucountry superfest.com

Summer and Autumn 2019

▶**New Orleans Pride** – early June - togetherwenola.com/pride
▶**Creole Tomato Festival** – mid-June
▶**Essence Festival** – early July - www.essence.com/festival
▶**Cajun-Zydeco Festival** – Music, theatre and dance events. Late June - www.jazzandheritage.org/cajun-zydeco
▶**New Orleans Film Festival** – mid-Oct - neworleansfilmsociety.org/festival

Maps

Photo credits

Page 4
French Market:© Paul Broussard/New Orleans Convention and Visitors Bureau
Jackson Square: © Gourmet Reise/New Orleans Convention and Visitors Bureau
Magazine Street: © Paul Broussard/New Orleans Convention and Visitors Bureau
City Park:© Paul Broussard/New Orleans Convention and Visitors Bureau
Audubon Park: © Rauluminate/iStockphoto.com

Page 5
Royal Street: © Zack Smith Photography/New Orleans Convention and Visitors Bureau
National WWII Museum: © Paul Broussard/New Orleans Convention and Visitors Bureau
Lafayette Cemetery: © Meinzahn/iStockphoto.com
Mardi Gras World: © Gourmet Reise/New Orleans Convention and Visitors Bureau
Frenchmen Street: © Patrick Frilet/hemis.fr

short-stay

- Charleston
- London
- New Orleans
- New York
- Paris

Visit your preferred bookseller for the short-stay series, plus Michelin's comprehensive range of Green Guides, maps, and famous red-cover Hotel and Restaurant guides.

THEGREENGUIDE short-stays New Orleans

Editorial Director	Cynthia Ochterbeck
Editor	Sophie Friedman
Contributing Writers	Cameron Todd
Production Manager	Natasha George
Cartography	Peter Wrenn, Nicolas Breton
Picture Editor	Yoshimi Kanazawa
Interior Design	Laurent Muller
Layout	Natasha George

Contact Us

Michelin Travel and Lifestyle North America
One Parkway South
Greenville, SC 29615
USA
travel.lifestyle@us.michelin.com

Michelin Travel Partner
Hannay House
39 Clarendon Road
Watford, Herts WD17 1JA
UK
✆01923 205240
travelpubsales@uk.michelin.com
www.viamichelin.co.uk

Special Sales

For information regarding bulk sales, customized editions and premium sales, please contact us at:
travel.lifestyle@us.michelin.com

Tell us
what you think
about our products.

Give us your opinion:

satisfaction.michelin.com

Michelin Travel Partner

Société par actions simplifiées au capital de 11 288 880 EUR
27 cours de l'Ile Seguin - 92100 Boulogne Billancourt (France)
R.C.S. Nanterre 433 677 721

ISBN 978-2-067230-21-7
Printed: April 2018
Printer: IME